GOSPEL
AND
SPIRIT

GOSPEL AND SPIRIT

Issues in New Testament Hermeneutics

GORDON D. FEE

Baker Academic

a division of Baker Publishing Group
Grand Rapids, Michigan

© 1991 by Gordon D. Fee

Published by Baker Academic
a division of Baker Publishing Group
P.O. Box 6287, Grand Rapids, MI 49516-6287
www.bakeracademic.com

Baker Academic edition published 2010
ISBN 978-0-8010-4622-3

Previously published in 1991 by Hendrickson Publishers

Printed in the United States of America

The Library of Congress has cataloged the original edition as follows:
Fee, Gordon D.
    Gospel and spirit: issues in new testament hermeneutics / Gordon D.
Fee
       p. cm.
    Includes bibliographical references.
    ISBN 10: 0-943575-78-8 (pbk.)
    ISBN 978-0-943575-78-0 (pbk.)
    1. Bible—Hermeneutics. 2. Hermeneutics—Religious aspects—Chris-
tianity. 3. Evangelicalism. 4. Pentecostalism. I. Title
BS476.F39 1991
220.6′01—dc20   91-32870

For:
Steve Hendrickson, David Townsley,
Patrick Alexander, and Phil Frank
of Hendrickson Publishers:
Former students, friends

TABLE OF CONTENTS

AUTHOR'S PREFACE

ON THE REASONS FOR THESE ESSAYS

Although my professional labors have primarily been in New Testament textual criticism and exegesis, hermeneutics has been my life-long passion. By hermeneutics I refer to the questions of the application of biblical texts—theologically and practically—to the life of the church and the individual. Since all hermeneutics is done within some frame of reference (see chapter 5), it is only fitting that I should herewith set forth the frame of reference and therefore the urgencies (even the casual reader will recognize that certain issues predominate) that both called forth these various essays in the first place and bring me now to gather them for publication in a single volume.

The twin focus in the title of this book indicates the context from within which these various essays emerged. As a New Testament scholar, born and raised in the Pentecostal tradition, I have spent nearly my whole adult life teaching and writing in the larger context of North American evangelicalism.

Although these two traditions have much in common, they also have some crucial points of differentiation. Therefore, even though I have lived through the years as a happy member of both traditions, at the same time it has been a situation not without tensions—in three directions.

would have required a considerable—and for me, a difficult—rewriting; it would also have caused them to lose some of their flavor, which for good or ill is part of my own oral style. The reader will also need to pardon a certain amount of repetition between/among some of the essays. I have added a considerable number of updating footnotes that do not appear in the original publications; these are enclosed in square brackets [ ] to distinguish them from the original material. If these papers have any further usefulness to the church in their present form, I shall be grateful to the Lord, for whose sake these various strugglings have ultimately been carried on.

Gordon D. Fee
Regent College
New Year's Day 1991

1

HERMENEUTICS AND COMMON SENSE: AN EXPLORATORY ESSAY ON THE HERMENEUTICS OF THE EPISTLES

It has long been my conviction that the battle for inerrancy must be settled in the arena of hermeneutics. The basic differences that have emerged among evangelicals, for example, between those who believe in "limited" or "unlimited" inerrancy[1] are not textual, but exegetical and hermeneutical. Unfortunately, a good deal of name-calling and mud-slinging has gone on over theological definitions of inerrancy, while exegetical and hermeneutical imprecision abounds.

This conviction has been supported most recently—unwittingly to be sure—by Harold Lindsell's *The Battle for the Bible*. Early on he inveighs against those who would "destroy the idea of biblical infallibility neatly by providing interpretations of Scripture at variance with the plain reading of the

---

[1] "Limited" inerrancy describes the belief that what God intends to convey in Scripture, or the message of Scripture, is without error, but that this absence of error does not necessarily apply to the incidental scientific or historical notations in Scripture. "Unlimited" inerrancy would include the latter items as well. This language, it should be noted, is the product of the latter group and is intended to exclude by definition of terms.

texts."[2] Yet when he himself tries to resolve "the case of the missing thousand" (Num 25:9; 1 Cor 10:8), he does so with precisely the same kind of hermeneutical stance, that is, by abandoning "the plain reading of the texts" and inveighing against those who read Paul's account "superficially" (pp. 167–69).[3]

The burden of this present essay is not necessarily to resolve the hermeneutical tensions highlighted by the battle for inerrancy. Nor does it aim to spell out the hermeneutical principles required by a belief in biblical inerrancy. Rather, the essay intends to be more foundational and to offer some suggestions in the area of common sense. The plea is for greater hermeneutical precision in order to answer the thorny question of how to move from the first to the twentieth century without abandoning the plain sense of the texts, on the one hand, and yet without canonizing first-century culture, on the other.

I have chosen to limit my remarks in this essay to the New Testament Epistles. The reason for this is twofold: (1) the problem of "cultural relativity" and its relationship to inerrancy is most often raised here. (2) Many of the battle lines in the current debate have been drawn over the issues of women's role in the twentieth-century church. Here especially, hermeneutical precision—or at least consistency—has been lacking on both sides. Unfortunately, in an area where hermeneutics is in fact the key issue, some have taken such a rigid stance on the basis of their own hermeneutics that they have accused others of believing in an errant Bible because they do not hold to the same interpretation.

I. The Basic Problem

In his now famous article on "Biblical Theology" in the *Interpreter's Dictionary of the Bible*, Krister Stendahl suggested the core of the hermeneutical problem today to be the

---

[2] Harold Lindsell, *The Battle for the Bible* (Grand Rapids: Zondervan, 1976) 30.
[3] [This is hermeneutical inconsistency of the worst kind. Lindsell's hermeneutics are clearly dictated by a theological a priori—a certain view of inerrancy. On the exegete's difficulty with this kind of thinking see the next chapter.]

contrast between "What did Scripture mean when it was written?" (the aim of historical exegesis) and "What does it mean to us today?" Historical exegesis, of course, is the culprit. By insisting that we go back to the then and there, many exegetes seemed less concerned with the here and now. Exegesis became a historical discipline, pure and simple; and the Bible seemed less a book for all seasons—an eternal word from God—and more like a book of antiquity, full of the culture and religious idiosyncrasies of another day. A new way of "hearing" Scripture was forced upon us. How is a statement spoken to a given historical context, in response to a specific historical problem, the word of God for us, whose context is so different? How, or when, does something that is culturally conditioned become transcultural?

These problems are especially acute for us in the evangelical tradition, where a real bifurcation has taken place. On the one hand, there are those who read the Epistles without a sense of the then and there. It is the eternal word, which is therefore always here and now. Yet in practice it works out a little differently. For example, many evangelicals consider the imperative to Timothy, "Use a little wine for the sake of your stomach" (1 Tim 5:23, RSV), to be culturally and specifically bound. Water was unsafe to drink, we are told, so Timothy was to take wine for medicinal reasons. All of this might be true, but many of the same Christians insist that men today should not have long hair, because "nature itself teaches us" this (although it is seldom recognized that short hair is "natural" only as the result of a non-natural means—a haircut!).[4] And we are never told how one arrives at such neat distinctions.

On the other hand, some of us who engage in historical exegesis do so at times with an uneasy conscience. We see a scholar like Ernst Käsemann engage in the same discipline with great expertise, but we are ill at ease with his "canon within the canon" (who decides on that inner canon?), which allows him to call the Gospel of John heterodox and say of Paul: "Being an apostle is no excuse for bad theology!" What is to keep us from the charge of picking and choosing when

[4] [Republishing this essay twelve years later reminds one how much hermeneutical issues are subject to the whims of cultural change!]

historical exegesis brings us face to face with statements and ideas that jar us in our twentieth-century ethos? How does the word spoken then and there, to which we are theologically committed, become a word to us today?

Because I am an exegete committed to the canon of Scripture as God's word, I can neither reject exegesis (what it meant then) nor neglect hermeneutics (what does it say today).[5] But those of us who take such a stance have still further problems: (1) In the past three decades there has been a spate of literature, mostly by Roman Catholics, on the *sensus plenior* of Scripture, which is defined by R. E. Brown as "the deeper meaning, intended by God but not clearly intended by the human author, that is seen to exist in the words of Scripture when they are studied in the light of further revelation or of development in the understanding of revelation."[6] Most evangelicals have avoided the term *sensus plenior*, since the concept of "development in the understanding of revelation" seems to leave the door open for the magisterium to define "God's intentions"; nonetheless, evangelicals use such terms as "secondary sense" to function in the same way as *sensus plenior*. The problem has to do with both the legitimacy of *sensus plenior* and, allowing its legitimacy, finding the principles for determining deeper meanings. (2) Protestant theologians have sometimes tended to lay aside the results of historical exegesis by distinguishing between the explicit and the implicit in Scripture, and they have argued: "Therefore not only the express statements of Scripture, but its implication . . . must be regarded as the word of God."[7] But again the rules or principles are seldom given as to how one finds the implications of the word of God.

---

[5] These are not precise usages of the two terms, but I will tend to use them in this way in the present essay. *Exegesis* is in fact concerned with what the text meant in its historical context. *Hermeneutics* has to do with the science of interpretation in all its ramifications. But since the term has to do especially with what a text means (which includes what is meant), I will use the term to refer to what the biblical text means for us in terms of our understanding and obedience.

[6] R. E. Brown, "Hermeneutics," in *The Jerome Bible Commentary* (Englewood Cliffs, N.J.: Prentice-Hall, 1968) 616.

[7] Louis Berkhof, *Principles of Biblical Interpretation* (2nd ed.; Grand Rapids: Baker, 1952) 159.

I have neither the space nor the expertise to answer all the questions that I have raised, but we evangelicals must speak to them. So here are some suggestions. I begin by stating in detail what exegesis of the Epistles as epistles entails, and then move on to the implications.

II. Interpreting the Epistles[8]

Traditionally for most Christians the Epistles seem to be the easiest parts of the New Testament to interpret. They are looked upon as so many propositions to be believed and imperatives to be obeyed. One need not be skilled in exegesis to understand that "all have sinned," or that "by grace are you saved through faith," or that "if any one is in Christ, he is a new creation." When we read, "Do all things without grumbling or questioning," our difficulty is not with understanding, but with obeying. How, then, do the Epistles as epistles pose problems for interpretation?

The answer to that quickly becomes obvious when one leads a group of Christians through 1 Corinthians. "How is Paul's opinion (e.g., 1 Cor 7:25: 'I have no command from the Lord, but I give a judgment as one who by the Lord's mercy is trustworthy,' NIV) to be taken as God's word?" some will ask, especially when they personally dislike some of the implications of that opinion. And the questions continue. How does the excommunication of the brother in chapter 5 relate to today's church, especially when he can simply go down the street to another church? What is the point of chapters 12–14, if one is in a local church where charismatic gifts are not accepted as valid for the twentieth century? How do we "get around" the very clear implication in 11:2–16 that women should have a head covering when they are praying and prophesying?

---

[8] [For many readers this section will be quite elementary, and in any case it appears in adapted form in Fee and Stuart, *How to Read*, as chapter 3. One may therefore wish to skip over to sections III and IV. I have included this section, as in the original essay, because much in the following essays assumes this material and some readers may wish to have it available for handy reference.]

It becomes clear that the Epistles are not as easy to interpret as is often thought. What principles, then, apply specifically to this genre? Here are some suggestions:

Let us begin by noting that the Epistles themselves are not homogeneous. Many years ago Adolf Deissmann, on the basis of the vast papyrus discoveries, made a distinction between "letters" and "epistles."[9] The former, the "real letters" as he called them, were nonliterary, that is, not written for the public and posterity, but "intended only for the person or persons to whom [they were] addressed." In contrast to this is the "epistle," which is "an artistic literary form, a species of literature . . . intended for publicity." Deissmann himself considered all the Pauline Epistles as well as 2 and 3 John to be "real letters."

Although William M. Ramsay cautioned us not "to reduce all the letters of the New Testament to one or other of these categories"[10]—in some instances it seems to be a question of more or less—the distinction is nevertheless a valid one. Romans and Philemon differ from one another not only in content but also in the degree to which they are occasional. And in contrast with any of Paul's letters, 1 Peter is far more an "epistle."

Further distinctions must also be drawn. For example, on the one hand, Hebrews is, as A. M. Hunter said, "three parts tract and one part letter."[11] But it is far more than a tract. It is an eloquent homily proclaiming the absolute superiority of Christ, interspersed with urgent words of exhortation. James, on the other hand, looks very little like a letter, but often very much like the wisdom literature of the Old Testament and Apocrypha, except that the wisdom literature is poetry and James is prose.

However diverse the Epistles might be, they nonetheless have one thing in common. They are occasional documents of the first century, written out of the context of the

---

[9] *Light from the Ancient East* (4th ed.; Grand Rapids: Baker, 1965 [reprint]) 146–245, esp. 228–45.
[10] *Letters to the Seven Churches of Asia* (New York: A. C. Armstrong and Son, 1905) 24.
[11] *Introducing the New Testament* (2nd ed.; London: SCM, 1957) 157.

author to the context of the recipients. We are often, as it were, on one side of a telephone conversation and must piece together from this end what the other party is saying or what the problem is. Or as R. P. C. Hanson said of 2 Corinthians: "As we read it, we sometimes feel as if we had turned the [radio on] in the middle of an elaborate play: characters are making most lively speeches and events of great interest and importance are happening, but we do not know who exactly the speakers are and we are not sure exactly what is happening."[12]

Moreover, all of this took place in the first century. Our difficulty here is that we are removed from them not only by so many years in time, and therefore in circumstances and culture, but also very often in the world of thought. Sound hermeneutics with regard to the Epistles, therefore, seems to require the following three steps:

1. The Original Setting

Understand as much as possible the original setting. The interpreter, if you will, must remove his or her twentieth-century bifocals, shedding the filter of twentieth-century mentality, and journey back into the first century. For the Epistles this has a double focus: (a) The interpreter must try as much as possible to reconstruct the situation of the recipients. That is, one must ask, how is this letter, or this section of the letter, an answer to their problems or a response to the recipients' needs? In every case, a primary concern of interpretation is to try to hear what they would have heard. (b) One must try to live with the author and understand his mentality and his context. Above everything else the interpreter must try to understand what the author intended the recipients to hear.

A maxim of hermeneutics for the Epistles is: The correct meaning of a passage must be something the author intended and the readers could have understood. For example, it has often been suggested that the phrase "when the perfect comes" (1 Cor 13:10) refers to the completion of the canon of Scripture, and that therefore it points to the end of the first century as the time when charismatic gifts will cease. But

[12] *II Corinthians* (London: SCM, 1954) 7.

surely that is altogether modern. Not only does the immediate context imply that the eschaton is intended (v. 12, "Now we see but a poor reflection as in a mirror; then we shall see face to face. Now I know in part; then I shall know fully, even as I am fully known," NIV), but there seems to be no way either that Paul could have meant the completion of the canon, or that the Corinthians would have so understood him.

2. The Word of God in the Original Setting

Hear the word of God that is addressed to that situation. This, of course, will be very closely tied to the first principle, and sometimes they will be one. The point here is not that some parts of the Epistles are inspired and others are not, but rather that the recipients' context often reflects a problem which needs correcting or a lack of understanding that needs enlightening. Our task is to discover (or "hear") the word of God that was addressed to that situation, the word that called for the recipients' obedience or brought them understanding.

3. The Word for Our Situation

Hear that same word as it is addressed to our situation. Understandably enough, most of us want to go directly to this step, that is, to have Paul speak directly out of the first century into ours. This is not to suggest that such may not or cannot happen, but the point is that very often the words of the Epistles are culturally conditioned by the first-century setting.[13] If these words are going to be God's word to us, then we must first of all hear what God's word was to the original recipients. By being aware of God's message both to the first century and to us, we avoid two dangers. First, there is the danger that the words may never leave the first century. Some passages seem to address us, and some do not. If we have no one struggling with whether to join pagan neighbors at feasts

---

[13] In a certain sense, of course, every word of Scripture is culturally conditioned, in that, for example, every word of the New Testament was first spoken in the context of the first century. The degree of "cultural conditioning" is a relative matter, which will receive attention later in this chapter.

in an idol's temple, or no one denying the bodily resurrection, or if our culture does not insist on women's heads being covered, or if we have no one drunk at the Lord's Table or shouting (by the "Spirit"), "Jesus is cursed," then the Epistles have historical interest at these points, but they scarcely address us.

The second danger is that the Epistles may never belong to the first century. In this case we suppose that every word comes directly to us. But sometimes that word is not God's intended word to us! For example, if the intent of Paul's word about partaking of the Lord's Supper "unworthily" is to correct the abuse of divisiveness based on a sociology of rich and poor while at the Lord's Table, then our ordinary application of that text to personal piety does not seem to be God's intended word. What was being said to that situation had to do with an attitude, or lack of it, toward the Supper itself. By their division and gluttony some of the Corinthians were profaning the Supper, not "discerning the body," missing the whole point of it all. Surely the twentieth-century Christian needs to hear that word, rather than a word about "getting rid of the sin in one's life in order to be worthy to partake," which is foreign to the point of the passage.

If we are to escape both of these dangers, then we must discover what God said to that setting, and it is that word which we must hear, even if we must hear it in a new setting or learn to recognize contemporary settings to which it should be addressed.

These principles may perhaps be best illustrated from a passage like 1 Corinthians 3:9b–17, which has been frequently misunderstood and misapplied, and has served as a theological battleground for a controversy to which Paul is not speaking at all.

It takes no great skill to recognize that the context of 1 Corinthians 3:9b–17 is partisan strife in the church at Corinth, carried on in the name of wisdom. In 1:10–12 Paul says that Chloe's people have told him all about the tendency to divide into cliques on the basis of favorite leaders. On either side of the immediate context (3:4–9a and 21–23) this strife is obviously still in view. Unless verses 9b–17 can be demonstrated to be a digression (and here they cannot), then one must assume them to speak directly to this problem.

Paul's response to the strife among the Corinthians is twofold. His first great concern is theological—their sloganeering and dividing on the basis of human leaders reflect on their understanding of salvation, as if humans (especially people with great wisdom and eloquence) had something to do with it. So in 1:18–2:16 Paul reaffirms that salvation is God's business from start to finish; and, as though deliberately to leave humans out of it, God wisely chose the foolishness of the cross as his means of accomplishing it, so that their trust (= "boast") will be not in men but in God.

In chapter 3 Paul turns to the practical implications of the divisions. He begins with two analogies intended to show the role of the human ministers in salvation. The particulars in both analogies are closely related (Paul plants/lays the foundation; Apollos waters/others build the superstructure; the Corinthian church is the field/building; God owns the field/building), but the point of each is considerably different. The agricultural analogy is intended to help the church have a proper perspective as to its leaders; they are servants, not lords. The figure from architecture (v. 10) turns the argument toward the present leadership; they are to take care how they build (the church is obviously the object being built). Verse 11 is simply a parenthesis reiterating the point of 1:18–2:16; namely, that Christ crucified is alone the foundation of the church in Corinth. Verses 12–15 therefore have nothing to do with personal morality or piety as to how one builds one's own life on Christ. Rather, this is Paul's charge to those who have responsibilities of building the church; and the point is, it is possible to build poorly! So let each one (those currently leading the church) take care how he or she builds. To have built with an emphasis on human wisdom or eloquence is to have built poorly, although the builder "himself will be saved, but only as through fire" (v. 15, RSV).

Within the same context Paul then turns the figure slightly and addresses the "building" (vv. 16–17)—and this is the real point of the section. He is not here writing about individual Christians, and especially not about the human body (a matter which he does address in a whole new context in 6:12–20). It is the whole church whom Paul addresses. They, especially when they are assembled, are God's temple, among whom God's Spirit dwells. If anyone destroys the temple, God will destroy that person! How were the Corinthians destroying the temple? By their prating "wisdom" as gospel and by their partisan strife, which inevitably would banish the Spirit.

If this then is the correct historical exegesis of this passage (and there seems to be no other), then what about step 2—What was God's word to the original recipients? First, there was a word to those who had "building" responsibilities, to build with care. Second, there was a word to the church, not to divide over human leaders. The church at Corinth was God's alternative to that city. To be divided was to destroy the church as God's option. Since it was in the church that God was gathering his new people, and in the church that he was now pleased to dwell, for the Corinthians to destroy that church was to put themselves under the prospect of fearful judgment.

III. The Hermeneutical Problems

We now come to the crux of the hermeneutical problem—step 3. What word does 1 Corinthians 3:9b–17 have for us? Here the exegete insists that when there are comparable particulars in our own time, then the word of God to us is precisely that which was spoken to the original recipients. There is still need for those with responsibilities in the church to take care how they build. It appears sadly true that the church has too often been built with wood, hay, or stubble, rather than with gold, silver, or precious stones; and such work, when tried by fire, has been found wanting. Furthermore, in this passage God addresses us as to our responsibilities to the local church. It must be a place where God's Spirit is known to dwell, and which therefore stands as God's alternative to the alienation, fragmentation, and loneliness of worldly society.

All of that seems easy enough. But now the real problems begin, problems for which I do not have ready answers, but for which I am prepared to suggest some directions for finding answers.

1. The Problem of Cultural Relativity

In the passage discussed above, step 3 was relatively easy because there are comparable particulars: we still have churches, which belong to God and which have various kinds of leaders. And we still have need to assess our leaders as servants, and the leaders still need to take care how they build, and the local church still should be a place so inhabited by the Spirit that it stands as God's alternative to its pagan surroundings.

But what of those sections of the Epistles which are also clearly responses to first-century occasions, but for which we do not seem to have comparable particulars? Or to put it back one step, How does one determine what is cultural and therefore belongs only to the first century, and what is transcultural and therefore belongs to every age.[14]

These questions are not easy to answer. Let us begin by noting the obvious: some things are clearly culturally conditioned, while others are just as clearly transcultural. For example, indicatives and imperatives such as, "Put on then, as God's chosen ones, holy and beloved, compassion, kindness, lowliness, meekness, and patience, forbearing one another and, if one has a complaint against another, forgiving each other" (Col 3:12–13, RSV), clearly transcend culture.[15] These are the "obvious" texts which seem to make the Epistles so easy to interpret.

On the other hand, for the Western world, the eating or noneating of food offered to idols is of no consequence. The only possible way, therefore, that we can find how 1 Corinthians 8–10 speaks to our situation is to go through the steps outlined above and "translate" the first-century situation into the twentieth century. To behave so as not to cause others to stumble and to avoid participating in what is demonic, which were God's word to the Corinthians, are just as surely God's word to us. Our problem is to recognize comparable culturally defined contexts. Before we turn to this problem in detail, we must first examine some guidelines for determining that which is culturally relative. With respect to these guidelines it

---

[14] In all candor it should be admitted that this last question is usually answered by our own cultural predisposition (see chapter 5 below). If we have been raised in a context where women pray, or prophesy, or teach, then 1 Tim 2:9–15 is seen as culturally conditioned. But if our context is more strictly patriarchal, then those words are seen as transcultural and as applicable to every situation.

[15] [See now chapter 3 below for a fuller explication of this matter.]

should be understood that not all "obvious" things will be equally obvious to all.[16]

a. One should first determine what is the central core of the message of the Bible and distinguish between that central core and what is dependent upon and/or peripheral to it. This is not to argue for a canon within the canon; rather, it is to safeguard the gospel from being transformed into law through culture and religious custom.

b. Similarly, one should note whether the matter in hand is inherently moral or nonmoral, theological or nontheological. Although some may differ with my judgments here, it would appear that eating marketplace food formerly offered to idols, requiring a head covering for women when they pray or prophesy, teaching in the church by women, and Paul's preference for celibacy are examples of issues not inherently moral. They may become so only by their use or abuse in given contexts. That is, eating in the pagan temple food which has been sacrificed to idols and teaching by a women who has usurped established authority (as would be true of men as well) become moral/ethical questions.

c. One must note further when the New Testament has a uniform witness on a given point and when there are differences within the New Testament itself. Thus, the corporate life of the community seems to be different in Acts 2–6 and 1 Corinthians,[17] and one should probably not make one the word of God over against the other. More difficult here, however, are the different attitudes toward food sacrificed to idols. Compare Acts 15:29 (21:25) and Revelation 2:14, 20, on the one hand, with what Paul says in 1 Corinthians 8–10, on the other.

---

[16] This is a collection of some of my own material with some suggestions from my colleague, David M. Scholer. The present arrangement is my own.

[17] The corporate life of the community in Acts 2–6 was not communal, but the sense of community was at a very high level. No one considered property to be one's own private possession; rather, it was made available for the whole community. In Corinth the church was composed of slaves and free (1 Cor 12:13; cf. 7:21–24). These distinctions apparently carried over to the Lord's Table, where the rich went ahead with their own meals and thus humiliated those who had nothing (11:21–22). Paul says they "have their own homes" in which to eat and drink (11:22, 34).

Our problem here is our lack of understanding of the terminology. Did it cover all the food which had been sacrificed to idols, including that sold in the marketplace, or did it refer specifically to eating such food in the pagan temples? If the former, Paul obviously reflects a more relaxed attitude.

d. One should be able to distinguish between principle and specific application. It is possible for a New Testament writer to support a relative application by an absolute principle and in so doing not make the application absolute. Thus in 1 Corinthians 11:2–16, the principle seems to be either (1) that one should do nothing to distract from the glory of God (especially by breaking convention) when the community is at worship or (2) that whatever else being God's eschatological people means in the present, it does not mean that the distinctions between the sexes have been eliminated. The specific problem seems to be relative, since Paul appeals to "custom" or "nature." Therefore, one may legitimately ask: "Would this have been an issue for us had we never encountered it in the New Testament documents?" If the specific problem were not relative, one might be tempted to argue that the culture in which any part of Scripture was given also becomes normative along with the principle itself.

e. One must keep alert to possible cultural differences between the first and twentieth centuries that are sometimes not immediately obvious. For example, to determine the role of women in the twentieth-century church, one should take into account that there were few educational opportunities for women in the first century, whereas such education is the expected norm in our society. This may affect our application of such texts as 1 Timothy 2:9–15.

f. Finally, one must exercise Christian charity at this point. Christians need to recognize the difficulties, to open the lines of communication with one another, to begin trying to define some principles, and to have love for and a willingness to ask forgiveness from those with whom they differ.

2. The Problem of Comparable
Context and Extended Application

Once one has determined that a passage is culturally relative, then if one is to hear the word of God at all, it must be "translated" into twentieth-century contexts in which that word is to be heard. Very similarly, even where step 3 has comparable particulars in the twentieth century, one must ask whether that is the only context to which that word can be addressed. Other questions inevitably arise: Are there limitations of applications? Are there principles as to what is legitimate in translating the first-century word into a new context? Let me suggest examples of problems which arise.

a. Second Corinthians 6:14–7:1 has often been used in Christian moral theology as a proof-text against Christians marrying non-Christians. But neither the immediate context nor the language of the passage suggests that this is the problem Paul is addressing. Probably Calvin is right—the text in its entirety repeats the injunction of 1 Corinthians 10:14–22,[18] that the Corinthians may not under any circumstances join their pagan friends at the idol's temple. Indeed, "what agreement is there between the temple of God and idols? For we are the temple of the living God." We simply have no context which is comparable. Into what kind of contexts, then, do we translate the principle, "Do not be yoked together with unbelievers"? And even if Calvin is wrong as to the particular historical context, it is surely true that this text is concerned with the community, not with individual believers. One may rightly question the legitimacy of transferring the context of this passage from the church and pagan temples to individual Christian and their marriages.[19]

b. First Corinthians 3:16–17, in speaking to the local church, presents the principle that what God has set aside for himself by the indwelling of his Spirit is sacred, and whoever destroys it will come under God's awful judgment. Again, is it legitimate to apply that text to the individual Christian or to the church universal in the same way it addresses the local community of believers? Is it really legitimate to argue from this text that God will judge the believer for abusing his body?

[18] See my own espousal of this position in "Ειδωλόθυτα Once Again—An Interpretation of 1 Corinthians 8–10," *Biblica* 61 (1980) 12–28.

[19] Although the point often made from this text is surely a proper one. However, such a point needs to be based on firmer ground than this one dubious text. It has to do finally with the complete incompatibility of "two becoming one" who cannot be one at the single crucial point of their relationship.

Similarly, 1 Corinthians 3:10–15 is addressing those with "building" responsibilities in the church, and warns of the loss they will suffer if they build poorly. Is it, then, legitimate to use this text, which speaks of judgment and salvation "as by fire," to illustrate the security of the believer?

If these are deemed legitimate applications, then the exegete would seem to have good reason to be nervous, for inherent in such "application" is the bypassing of historical exegesis altogether. After all, to apply 1 Corinthians 3:16–17 to the individual believer is precisely what the church has erroneously done for centuries. Why do exegesis at all? Why not simply begin at step 3 and fall heir to centuries of error?

The exegete, therefore, would argue for two principles: (1) in "translating" from the first-century context to another, the two contexts must be genuinely comparable.[20] We may not all agree, of course, on our definition of the "genuinely comparable," but surely that must be the legitimizing factor. What addresses the local church speaks to the individual only as he or she is related to what God is saying to the whole. Therefore, it is not legitimate to apply 1 Corinthians 3:16–17 to the individual in the same way it applies to the assembly—unless he or she is the one destroying the assembly as God's alternative by divisiveness! On the other hand, 2 Corinthians 6:14–7:1 may apply to the individual in a circuitous way, since it was as individuals that the church was "unequally yoked" to pagan temples. But even here it is better to approach the text from the standpoint of the community.

(2) Usually the "extended application" is seen to be legitimate because it is otherwise true; that is, it is clearly spelled out in other passages where it is the intent. If that be the case, then one should go to those other passages and stop abusing texts where it is not the intent. If there are no such passages where it is the intent, then one may legitimately ask whether that can truly be the word of God which one learns only by "extended application."

---

[20] R. E. Brown, "Hermeneutics," uses the term *homogeneity* to express this same principle. What fails to have "homogeneity," he styles "accommodation."

3. The Problem of "Implication" and "Sensus Plenior"

I am here lumping together several problems which have one thing in common: Scripture is often used in such a way as to say more than was the primary intention of the human author. R. E. Brown would call these "more-than-literal" senses; however, I would also include here those things that are explicit in the text, but incidental to the author's primary intention.

a. The exegete who is doing his or her work properly is forever asking the question: But what is the point? What is the author driving at? That is, one is always raising the question of the author's intent. At the same time, it is to be hoped that one is also asking questions about the content, questions of lexicography, syntax, background, and so forth. Further, one is also wary of over-exegeting—for example, finding something that would stagger the author were he informed someone had found it in his writing, or building a theology upon the use of prepositions, or discovering meaning in what was not said.

But because the exegete is so intent on intent, that is, on finding the author's point, the interpreter often comes to the text with a different agenda from that of the theologian, whose concerns are more often the content and its theological implications. An excellent case in point might be 1 Thessalonians 3:11: "Now may our God and Father himself, and our Lord Jesus, clear the way. . . ."

The exegete does not neglect the fact that the sentence has a compound subject and singular verb, but neither is the interpreter tempted to make too much theological hay out of it. The point is, Paul is not here trying to make a theological statement as to the unity of the Father and Son. He is concerned with returning to Thessalonica, a concern which he articulates in prayer. The exegete wants to discover why Paul shows such concern, and how that affects other things said in the epistle; the exegete wants to know what word there is from God to us in the wish-prayer of an apostle to a neophyte congregation in Thessalonica.

But the exegete must not, indeed dare not, overlook the theological implications of the prayer, which assumes the Father and the Son to act in unity. What is not intentionally theological is nonetheless incidentally theological; and even though it is incidental, it is not thereby unimportant or any less the word of God. It is hoped the exegete and theologian differ here only in the primary interest each brings to the text.

b. What has been said above as to "extended application" continues to hold true here. What is determined to be true by implication is so on the basis of the analogy of Scripture. That is, it is either taught clearly elsewhere, or it can be shown by numerous examples to be the human author's theological assumptions or presuppositions.

It is precisely for this reason that one must reject the Mormon application of 1 Corinthians 15:29. In spite of some exegetical gymnastics arguing for the contrary, the clear implication of that text is that some Corinthians were practicing baptism of the dead. I am of the mind that the passage implies that Paul is not terribly shaken by the practice. But the analogy of Scripture scarcely allows us to regard such a practice as either mandatory or repeatable by later Christians, for neither by implication nor by explication do we have the faintest idea as to the particulars of that baptism—for whom, by whom, for what reasons, and with what significance. Here is a place where the point of the text is clear: in a purely ad hoc argument, Paul says that the practice argues for a future resurrection; otherwise what these Corinthians are doing is absurd. But what in fact they were doing remains a singular mystery belonging to first-century Corinth.

c. A final point here. The apparent identification of Jesus with the Spirit in 2 Corinthians 3:17 ("Now the Lord is the Spirit") has long been a *crux interpretum* for exegetes and theologians. Along with 1 Corinthians 15:45 this passage seems to lend credence to a kind of Spirit Christology, as if for Paul the risen Lord and the Spirit are one and the same (so Hans Lietzmann). But as a matter of fact, what seems to be implied rather strongly is not said by Paul at all. The point is, sound exegesis will often correct erroneous inferences, and such inferences must always be subject to exegesis.

In the passage at hand, Paul has been glorying in his privilege of ministry in the new covenant, a covenant brought on by the coming of the Spirit and contrasted with the covenant of the letter, which led to death. To illustrate the greater glory of this new covenant he inserts a pesher (a special kind of Jewish commentary) on Exodus 34:29–34. He concludes by citing Exodus 34:34, with slight changes, so as to move it from Moses to the present. Thus, "whenever anyone [not Moses only] turns to the Lord, 'the veil is taken away' "(2 Cor 3:16, NIV). Now "the Lord" being referred to in this passage, Paul goes on to say, "is the Spirit," the life-giving Spirit of the new covenant; and where the Spirit of the Lord is, there is liberty (= the freedom of the new covenant, freedom from the law with its imposition of death). The passage, therefore, is a pneumatological one, not christological, and it is not identifying Christ and the Spirit, even by implication.

But is it not possible that there is a *sensus plenior*, a deeper or secondary meaning to such texts? After all, taken by itself, 2 Corinthians 3:17 does use language to identify Christ with the Spirit. Is it not possible that God intended something quite beyond what the human author intended? Besides, we have the example of the New Testament writers, who, in exegeting the Old Testament, found *sensus plenior*. Is it not possible on such grounds that those people are right who argue that "the perfect" in 1 Corinthians 13:10 does indeed mean canon?

Some observations and personal opinions: (1) There is inherent danger in the concept of *sensus plenior*. If indeed God intends something beyond what the human author intended—and I would certainly not deny that possibility—then who speaks for God? That is, who determines the deeper meaning God intends for us? The magisterium? The Dispensationalist's view of history? I admit to being squeamish regarding the whole area.

(2) The fact that the New Testament writers found *sensus plenior* in the Old Testament does not help me much. R. N. Longenecker has argued, and I tend to agree, that we cannot repeat the exegesis of the New Testament writers, precisely because what they did at that point was inspired.[21] In this case we know God's fuller meaning in the Old Testament because he revealed it through the New Testament writers. But this can scarcely serve as a model for the twentieth century, any more than Paul's use of pesher and allegory can. We belong to a different hermeneutical world.

(3) There is for me the possibility of a *sensus plenior* in predictive prophecy. But if so, it would seem to be something

[21] In *Biblical Exegesis in the Apostolic Period* (Grand Rapids: Eerdmans, 1975) esp. 205–20.

available to us only after the fact, not before. Therefore, I would tend to hold such interpretations in abeyance.

(4) All of this leads me to suggest that a *sensus plenior* in the Epistles is not a solid option, except perhaps where the writer is engaging in predictive prophecy.

IV. Some Concluding Remarks

How, then, is all of this concern for greater precision in the exegesis and hermeneutics of the Epistles related to the battle of inerrancy? In several ways, I think.

Even if one is uncomfortable with my special use of the terms, the distinction I have made between exegesis and hermeneutics is a very important one. The first task of the interpreter is to discover what the text meant when it was originally written. The question of the inerrancy and trustworthiness of Scripture must be carried on at that level, not at the level of "what does the text mean for us today." This is not a way of trying to get around anything. In fact a careful reading of this paper will indicate that quite the opposite is my intent. All of Scripture is God's word. The hermeneutical task is to free the word to speak to our own situation.

My point here is a crucial one. We simply must be done with the nonsense that suggests that some evangelicals are "soft on Scripture" because, for example, they believe in women's ministries in the church. One may as well accuse B. B. Warfield of not believing in inerrancy because he had a hermeneutical way to get around Paul's very clear command to seek spiritual gifts, especially prophecy. The so-called women's issue is a hermeneutical question, and we will have differences here. But those differences are not questions of the authority of Scripture. They are questions of interpretation, and have to do with our historical distance from the text and the whole question of cultural relativity. We will not all agree on the principles I have suggested. But surely we must agree that hermeneutics is the arena in which we must carry on the discussion, not in the arena of the doctrine of Scripture per se.

If the battle of inerrancy must be carried on at the exegetical level—and it must—then we simply cannot afford to play loose with the text at that point.

Here is one of the great weaknesses in Harold Lindsell's book, for example. Through a series of contrived interpretations he does things to the biblical text that good exegetical method must vigorously oppose as an abuse of the text.

A case in point. In order to reconcile some apparent difficulties between the Synoptic and Johannine accounts of Peter's denials, Lindsell argues that Peter really denied Jesus six times! It may be argued, by sheer sophistry, that for the biblical writer to say three does not exclude the possibility of six, because six can also include any number up to six. But that is to play havoc with the clear intent of the biblical writers who clearly say that there would be three denials. To turn that three into six by a kind of hermeneutical harmony in the fashion of Tatian's heretical Diatessaron borders on arguing for an errant text. I remember a day in 1975 when Fred Lynn of the Boston Red Sox batted in ten runs in a single game. Had a reporter for the Boston *Globe* written that Lynn batted in five runs, the reporter would not technically have been in error, for Lynn did in fact bat in five runs. But not a person in Boston who saw the game would have been convinced that the sportswriter was not really in error. For the clear intent of such reporting is not to give part of the whole, but the whole itself.

Furthermore, to say that God really meant six when the word clearly says three seems to contravene the nature of God and his revelation. It is to argue that God intended to obfuscate rather than to reveal or make plain. Exegesis, therefore, must be carried on with precision.

Since inerrancy must be wrestled with at the exegetical level, the real question in the debate is not so-called limited inerrancy. Rather, it has to do with the amount of accommodation one believes the Holy Spirit allowed the human authors.

That there is some accommodation one can scarcely deny. The very fact that God chose to give his word in ordinary human language, through real people, in real historical settings, is an expression of this accommodation.

Thus, the Bible is not just a collection of sayings or propositions from God, written in a unique, divine language. God did not say, "Learn these truths: Number 1. There is no God but one, and I am he. Number 2. I am the creator of all things, including humankind." And so on. These propositions are indeed true, and they are found in the Bible. A collection of such propositions might have made things easier for us, to be sure! But God chose to speak his word through a wide range of literary forms (narrative histories, chronicles, law codes, dramas, all kinds of poems, proverbs, prophetic oracles, parables, stories, letters, Gospels, and apocalypses). Each of these is a different kind of human speech, and each requires its own special rules for interpretation.[22]

There is also a wide range of people who were used by the Holy Spirit to write Scripture. Thus we can distinguish between the way Paul and John express themselves theologically as well as between their grammar and literary style. To say they differ in expression is not to say that they are opposed, or that one of them is in error.

Another expression of accommodation is to be found in the fourfold Gospel. People like Tatian and some well-meaning modern authors have always been embarrassed by that reality and attempt to harmonize the four into one. But it was God who inspired the four. We do well to keep it that way. The fact that the Aramaic words that Jesus originally spoke are now recorded for us in Greek translation is already an accommodation. So also is the fact that his words as they are recorded in one Gospel are not usually duplicated exactly in the others.

Such expressions of accommodation are accepted by all evangelicals, and even by some fundamentalists. The real problem here is, where do we draw the line? The differences that exist among evangelicals are basically a matter of finding a starting point. Do we start with a theological a priori and say what God must do, or do we start with the text itself and say what God did do? As an exegete my sympathies obviously lie with the latter option.[23]

Take, for example, the question of whether accommodation allows for the human author to speak popularly, even if such speech is not precise, according to modern scientific norms. The exegete sees Jesus speaking popularly in Matthew

---

[22] [See now *How to Read the Bible for All Its Worth* (with Douglas Stuart; Grand Rapids: Zondervan, 1982).]
[23] [For a further elaboration of the concerns in this paragraph see now chapter 2 below.]

13:32 when he says that the mustard seed "is the smallest of all your seeds" (NIV). But if one argues a priori that every botanical allusion in Scripture must carry the precision of the twentieth-century botanist, then one must resort once again to remote possibilities that are improbable in the highest degree.[24]

I do not wish to resolve this issue here, for that would require a paper of much greater length [see the next chapter]. However, these are the kinds of questions that must form a part of the discussion; and no philosophical or emotional a priori should be allowed to prejudge how the believer in biblical inerrancy must decide these questions.

Finally, I will contend for one thing above all. The occasional nature of the New Testament Epistles is scarcely debatable. This does indeed give us many and varied exegetical and hermeneutical problems. But the fact that they are occasional is also their greater glory. Instead of trying to circumvent that reality by a variety of hermeneutical ploys, we should affirm with thanksgiving that the weakness of God is stronger than men and the foolishness of God is wiser than men. The same God who spoke his living word most eloquently through the weakness of an incarnation, has also spoken his written word through the weakness of human language and human history. That this word was spoken once is precisely what gives us the courage to believe it will so speak again and again despite the relativities and ambiguities of history and culture. The eternal word never changes, even though the historical circumstances in which it speaks are ever subject to change.

[24] On this issue Lindsell allows for the possibility of accommodation (*Battle for the Bible*, 169), but it also seems clear that he would prefer not to have to make this allowance.

2

THE EVANGELICAL DILEMMA: HERMENEUTICS AND THE NATURE OF SCRIPTURE[1]

Some years ago my then colleague David Scholer received a letter from a former student, who was in pastoral ministry in downtown Boston. In the course of her letter, she remarked, "I have come to realize that above everything else the ministry is hermeneutics." That was a profound insight that I have had reason to reflect on again and again. What she meant, of course, was that Christian ministry means always to be thinking about and reflecting on Scripture in such a way that one brings it to bear on all aspects of human life.

Precisely because this is so, one does nothing more important in the formal training for Christian ministry than to wrestle with hermeneutics: the meaning and application of Scripture. But at the same time, precisely because it impacts all that one does and thinks with regard to Christian faith, it is important that one learn to do it well—and consistently.

In the previous essay[2] I hinted at the possibility that the debate over inerrancy would end up being not over the *text* of Scripture, but over its *interpretation*. Subsequent events,

---

[1] [For the origins of this essay see Author's Preface. Since thislecture in particular was originally prepared for a seminary audience, some of the trappings of that audience still remain.]

[2] [Which was written in 1978 and published in 1980.]

such as Summit II of the International Council on Inerrancy and the expulsion of Robert Gundry from the Evangelical Theological Society, seem to have borne that out. The issue is only partly Scripture itself; the real issue is hermeneutics—what some think is *allowable* within an evangelical context as to the meaning and application of the text. May women be ordained or not? Is there evidence of editorial activity among the Gospel writers or not? May practicing homosexuals be ordained to Christian ministry or not? These are the urgent questions, and they are *not* decided by inerrancy (although some have certainly tried to do so), but at the hermeneutical level.

Since I stand squarely within historic orthodoxy—and therefore also within historic evangelicalism—on the doctrine of Scripture, and yet since by ecclesiastical tradition and by temperament I find myself standing on the outside of the debate over inerrancy, it seemed to me to be a worthwhile exercise to try my own hand at finding an evangelical hermeneutics. I realize how arrogant that may sound. I do not, however, contend that what I present here is *the* way for evangelicals to go. I offer it rather as *an* alternative within evangelicalism, and I would like to submit it to the marketplace for discussion and review.

My ultimate concern is to test some ideas on the whole question as to how we handle the New Testament imperatives, so that we establish a hermeneutics that, on the one hand, calls for genuine obedience to Christ, yet, on the other hand, is more consonant with the gospel itself, rather than with some form of law. But in order to get to that concern, in this present essay I want to do two things: (1) define what I perceive as the central urgency in an evangelical hermeneutics—how to speak hermeneutically from one's doctrine of Scripture itself; and (2) point out the hermeneutical problem areas for an evangelical doctrine of Scripture.

I. Words, Communication, and Meaning

In order to get at my concerns I want to start way back—with the need itself.

Human speech, by its very nature (i.e., the use of symbols [words] to convey meaning), requires hermeneutics. When we speak we tend to think it rather straightforward: *my* thoughts, expressed in words common to both of us, heard by *your* ears, and recorded and deciphered by *your* minds. Unfortunately, however, we have all experienced the phenomenon of being misunderstood, and thereby know what a precarious business human speech can be. Perhaps you have seen the wall plaque that reads: "I know you believe you understand what you think I said, but I am not sure you realize that what you heard is not what I meant." The problem, of course, is that between the mind of the speaker and that of the hearer are symbols—chiefly words, sometimes inflections or body language.

There is, therefore, probably a degree of misunderstanding between any two or more people engaged in an extended conversation or dialogue. That degree is increased as several factors are added. For example, short dialogue between two people who know each other well usually has the highest degree of understanding, especially since dialogue itself allows for clarification. But the possibility of *mis*understanding is increased as one is distanced from his or her hearer or reader, such as with monologue replacing dialogue, or when the speaker is unknown to the hearer(s), or when writing replaces speaking. As one adds other distancing factors, especially time, culture, and a second language, the possibility of misunderstanding is heightened the more, unless the writer has tried to be particularly sensitive to such distancing factors; but even then the degree of understanding is predicated for the most part on the degree of common experience. Such complexities in communication should give guest preachers and lecturers, and especially the writers of books, plenty of reason to pause.

It is this last factor—our distance from the biblical writers in time and culture—that demands that we become good exegetes, if we are truly to understand the meaning of Scripture. We must wrestle with *their* use of words, syntax, and literary forms, which express *their* ideas, and we must hear those ideas within both the author's and the readers' cultural contexts and presuppositions, if ever we are adequately to understand what they intended by their words.

But that is only one part of the task, and frankly it is one that believer or unbeliever alike can engage in with a relative degree of objectivity, although we recognize of course that any interpreter always brings to a text a considerable amount of cultural baggage and personal bias. But a relative degree of objectivity should be possible whether one has either supernatural or non-supernatural presuppositions. One may or may not believe that Jesus rose from the dead, but no serious exegete can deny that *Paul* believed it, or that he believed there would also be a future resurrection of believers. Thus this task is the more strictly historical one. Whether one is a good exegete or not will depend on the right blend of knowledge of the primary sources, sensitivity to historical possibilities, and good common sense (my way of talking about evaluating historical probabilities).

The other side of the task, however, and for the interpretation of Scripture the urgent one, is that of relevance. How do these ancient texts have meaning for us today, or do they? At this point nearly *everything* depends on the presuppositions of the interpreter. Here is where evangelical and liberal divide, where Pentecostal and Dispensationalist, or Baptist and Presbyterian, part company. And here is where hermeneutics for a believer or nonbeliever, for a Christian or a Christian Scientist —even though they are reading the same texts—means radically different things. Many evangelicals, of course, tend to think the answer lies in finding the meaning of the text itself; and sometimes that is true. But far more often it is not so. Simply witness, for example, how almost anyone would agree on Paul's intent in 1 Cor 14:40 that the Corinthians in their situation should not, in light of Paul's words in chapter 14, forbid speaking in tongues; yet how many would differ from a Pentecostal like myself as to whether that admonition applies in a local church today.

What the text *means*—that is, *how* it is a word for *us*—that is the crucial hermeneutical question. Since our presuppositions determine so much at this point, let us therefore examine the basic presupposition that will distinguish an evangelical Protestant from other expressions of Christianity as well as from other religious expressions or attitudes, namely, the nature of Scripture.

II. Scripture and the Nature of Religious Authority

To this point I have purposely referred to the biblical documents as Scripture. That in itself is a commitment to religious authority that distinguishes Christian from non-Christian. But what it means to call these documents Scripture is not shared equally by all Christians. Here the evangelical Protestant and the traditional Roman Catholic have much in common over against liberal Protestantism or Catholic Modernism. The distinction between the evangelical Protestant and traditional Roman Catholic lies at a different point—the nature of authority itself.

What, then, does it mean *for us* to name as Scripture these documents that were written in recognizable human language, in largely recoverable historical contexts of a roughly 1500–year span some 1900–plus years ago?

That leads us to articulate a few presuppositions about the nature of religious authority in general, before particularizing on the evangelical's understanding of religious authority.

I begin with some preliminary observations:

(1) The question of religious authority, most would agree, is an ultimate one; and ultimately we are dealing with God himself. The problems lie with the penultimates, i.e., how God communicates or reveals himself; or what authoritatively mediates God and God's will to humankind.

(2) It should be noted further that one's basic authority is ultimately a matter of faith, i.e., one makes a faith commitment of some kind that says: "This plus this," or "This not that," has authority in my life or church. This is so even if one does not articulate it.

(3) Related to this is the reality that one cannot finally *prove* his or her authority to be the correct one. What one can hope to show is the reasonableness of it. Thus, for example, just as a historian cannot prove the resurrection of Jesus, but can nonetheless show how the resurrection seems to make the best sense of all the available historical data, so I cannot prove the Bible to be God's word. But one can show by a variety of evidence that it makes good sense to believe it to be so.

As to religious authority itself, then, it should be noted that it is of two kinds: Either (1) it is *external* to oneself (so-called objective authority), or (2) it is *internal* (so-called subjective). External authority is basically of three kinds: (a) a sacred book, (b) an authoritative person(s) [sometimes = the founder], or (c) a community of persons [sometimes = tradition]. Internal authority is of two kinds: reason and experience.

Each of these has its problem areas. For external authority it is always a question of authentication: why this one and not another. The problem with internal authority is that it lacks any means of verification, or absoluteness. People with similar religious experience or a common view of reason may find support in one another, but the ultimate authority lies with oneself—it is *my* experience, after all, or *my* reason—and the result is the autonomy of the individual. It is this idolatry, the autonomy of reason and the individual—which reflects a failure to take the Fall seriously enough—that divides the Christian from most Western non-Christians as well as the evangelical from the liberal.

The evangelical stance on the question of religious authority is that our basic authority is external. This is predicated on the prior theological grounds (which we find eminently reasonable) of the nature of God and the reality of the Fall. We believe that our vision of God was distorted by the Fall and therefore that God cannot be *discovered*, that is, he cannot be known from below, as it were. God must reveal himself if he is to be known at all; our knowledge must come from above. We further believe that God has so revealed himself: by deeds, in a Person, and through a book that both reports and interprets those deeds and that Person. Because ultimately we know the Person, or hear the gospel, through the book, we take the book to be our primary penultimate authority. That is, we believe that this is the way God chose to reveal and to communicate. The other forms of authority (tradition, reason, experience) in various ways authenticate, verify, or support, but all must themselves finally be authenticated by Scripture.

As an aside, my own understanding of Roman Catholicism is that they would also affirm that Scripture should authenticate other authority. The problem seems to be that whenever that attempt breaks down, they allow tradition, not Scripture, to have the final word.[3]

Because of the conviction as to the ultimate revelatory nature of Scripture, the church has traditionally tried to find ways to verbalize this conviction so as to safeguard it from being watered down, either from one of the other kinds of

[3] [On this question, see chapter 5.]

authority on the one hand, or from the drifts of culture or collective fallenness on the other. Out of such concern arose our various attempts to articulate the doctrine of the inspiration of Scripture by the Holy Spirit. By this articulation we were addressing first the problem of authentication: Because Scripture is ultimately inspired by the Spirit of God, Scripture is understood to be self-authenticating. In the final analysis, we believe that the authority is intrinsic. God has spoken—and will continue to speak—here. Let the lion out of the cage; it will defend itself.

Second, by the doctrine of inspiration we were articulating our conviction that God himself is the ultimate source of the Christian faith, as it is revealed or defined in our sacred book.

III. The Nature of Evangelical Hermeneutics

That leads us then, finally, to look at the specific nature of evangelical hermeneutics, how it differs from others, and what are its own inherent tensions or difficulties.

It is the doctrine of inspiration, that God inspired not only the people who spoke but also the words they spoke, that distinguishes the evangelical view of Scripture, and also forces us to wrestle with the issues of hermeneutics. Inspiration maintains that God indeed "spoke all these words and said. . . ." But it does not maintain that he *dictated* all these words. To the contrary it recognizes, indeed argues, that these words are also the words of people in history. Thus our understanding of the nature of Scripture is that *the Bible is God's word spoken in human words in history.*[4] As God's word it has eternal relevance; he addresses us. It is ours to hear and obey. But as human words in history the eternal word has historical particularity. None of the words was spoken in a vacuum. Rather they were all addressed to, and conditioned by, the specific historical context in which they were spoken.

Evangelical hermeneutics, therefore, by its very understanding of the *nature* of Scripture, must always be interacting with the intersection of the human and divine in these words that are believed also to be *the* word. As such it must struggle

---

[4] This is adapted from G. E. Ladd. See *The New Testament and Criticism* (Grand Rapids: Eerdmans, 1967) 12.

against the tendency to come down on either side (the human or the divine) in such a way as effectively to negate the other.

Let me illustrate. First, an evangelical sympathizes with, but finally rejects, the fundamentalist's anxiety over the need for *absolute* authority, which tends thereby to replace the authority of the word with the authority of the interpreter. To arrive at such an absolute the fundamentalist tends to see Scripture as a divine word *only*, and thus merely pays lip service to its human authors. As with Docetists or Apollinarians in Christology, the word may appear to be human, or even to have physical attributes of humanity, but in reality the divine has been so superimposed on the human as to eliminate it almost altogether as being truly human.

On the other hand, secondly, the evangelical also sympathizes with, but usually much less so and finally rather totally rejects, the liberal's fear of imposing rules upon the church in the name of God that seem more arbitrary than loving, or dogmas that are difficult for moderns to swallow. But here, as with Arian Christology, the error lies in an affirmation of the human that diminishes or negates altogether the divine. Not all of our fear on this side may be fair or well-grounded, but it does seem to be a legitimate one. All too often the emphasis on the human side of Scripture results in the hearing of *a* word from *man* more than *the* word of *God*. In Scripture God does not so much speak to people, as people are speaking to and about him. The result is what James Smart called "the strange silence of the Bible in the church,"[5] a failure of "thus saith the Lord," but plenty of "I think," "I maintain," or "it seems to me."

The evangelical response to such hermeneutics is still valid. First, such an attitude toward Scripture tends to divest it of its divine authority. Rather than a powerful word from God that addresses us all and sits in ultimate judgment on our impoverished human lives, what is left of Scripture are the meager results of Western rationalism with its pallid moralism and a historical criticism that sits in heavy judgment on the text itself. If I select only parts of Scripture as God's word, if I create a canon within the canon, if I listen only to what is

[5] See his book by this title (Philadelphia: Westminster, 1970).

compatible with contemporary fallenness—even if I do it in the name of love or broadmindedness—how does God himself, who judged human wisdom as folly through the scandal of the cross, how does God speak his judgments on our present fallenness, and do it with any authority? He speaks only what we think he should speak, only what is palatable to certain political or economic convictions, or finally only what *we* allow him to say. The final word and judgment are ours. That seems to us to be too great a price to pay to be contemporary or incarnational or "loving." The scriptural view is that one must speak the *truth* in love.

Furthermore, the evangelical is always puzzled by the liberal, who redirects authority from the word itself to the interpreter of the word, as to why he or she still wants to use Scripture at all. Why bother with the text of the Bible, when the final judgment rests with us? The answer to that, of course, is the Bible's historic place in the Christian faith and the fact that one has judged it to have a great deal of wisdom and truth after all! So one goes to it, and picks and chooses from it, but there is no thundering voice from Sinai, nor very little of the prophetic finger calling us into question—"Thou are the man"—or if there is, it tends to lack final authority from the outside. So we feel compelled to reject this hermeneutical stance that sees Scripture as a human word in such a way as to blunt or negate its also being God's very word. Just as we also feel compelled to reject the stance that sees it as a divine word in such a way as to divest it of its truly human character.

But to steer between these two polarities is not without its own difficulties. To see Scripture as *both* human and divine creates its own set of tensions.

First, the intersection of the eternal word with historical particularity leaves us with far more ambiguities than some feel comfortable with. What do we do with the holy war and the slaughter of nations? How do we reconcile the lament to have Babylonian children's heads bashed against rocks with God's abundant mercy? What do we do with the holy kiss, charismatic gifts, head coverings, the mode of baptism, the sovereignty of God and human freedom, to name but a few items where evangelicals, who all hold the *same* view of Scripture, are deeply divided as to how it impacts our lives at specific points?

The longing for absoluteness on all matters, which compels the fundamentalist mindset, is ever with the evangelical as well—precisely because of the conviction that Scripture is *God's* word above all. Since God himself is unseen and known only by revelation and faith, and must finally be trusted, the need for certainty is often vested in the penultimate that leads us to God. Such a need drove the Pharisee to put a hedge around the law and the legalist to put a hedge around certain behavior. It is too much to trust in God without absolute certainty, which of course, as Bultmann rightly criticized us, is its own form of idolatry.

Hence there is always pressure from this side of our fallenness to eliminate ambiguity. If God himself is infallible, then the text of his word must be infallible. If the text is infallible, then there must be an infallible understanding of it. But that is *not* an evangelical syllogism. The text itself in its intent is infallible, we would argue, because of its character as God's word. And we insist on this, because even if we disagree on the meaning of the text, our hope lies in the text itself to have its inherent power as God's word to correct us.

But the buck stops there, at the text and its intent, as to what is infallible. God did not choose to give us a series of timeless, non-culture-bound theological propositions to be believed and imperatives to be obeyed. Rather he chose to speak his eternal word *this* way, in historically particular circumstances, and in every kind of literary genre. God himself, by the very way he gave us this word, locked in the ambiguity. So let us not fight God and insist that he give us his word another way, or as we are more apt to do, rework his word along theological or cultural prejudgments that turn it into a minefield of principles, propositions, or imperatives, but denude it of its ad hoc character as truly human. The ambiguity is a part of what God did in giving us his word *this* way. Our task is to recognize and capitalize on what God has done.

Second, the fact of Scripture's historical particularity not only locks in a degree of ambiguity, but also brings with it a degree of accommodation.[6] Here too is an area of evangelical anxiety. That there is *some* accommodation is a matter on

[6] [See chapter 1 above, pp. 20–23.]

which all agree—even the fundamentalist, albeit sometimes unwittingly. But how much, and of what kind(s), these are the burning questions. Could God, or did God, inspire midrash, for example, or pseudepigraphy? Or, would God *not* give us four Gospels if they were to disagree, as a student once insisted? Do the differences and so-called discrepancies reflect accommodation, or must they always have a resolution that satisfies Western logic?

Here is where some sore spots among evangelicals are openly festering; unfortunately they tend to fester between exegetes and dogmaticians. The issue is whether one is wont to begin with a theological a priori and conform historical questions to that a priori (= telling the exegetes what God could or could not have done even before one looks at the data), or whether one starts with historical investigation and expresses one's theological constructs in light of that investigation (= telling the theologian what God in light of historical probabilities seems to have done). The believing exegete and theologian, it should be noted, are both working within a circle, hopefully the same circle. The tensions, therefore, lie not only in the starting point, but also in how much flexibility each thinks the circle can bear—either in or out.

One of the difficulties here is related to our reading these texts from our own cultural perspectives. The Western mind, for example, seems far more concerned with precision as the only way that "truth" can be expressed than did basically oral cultures. It is not that they played fast and loose with events per se, but that they appear to be far less concerned with verbatim reporting or the precise nature of all details.

Third, inherent to the conviction that Scripture is both human and divine is the recognition that it has diversity within an essential unity. The diversity results from its historical particularities; the unity from its ultimately divine origins. But how to articulate this unity and diversity is another area in which evangelicals are not all agreed. Unfortunately, it is also another area where exegetes and dogmaticians are all too often at odds.

The traditional hermeneutical principle here is the *analogy of Scripture*—Scripture interprets Scripture, because God is its ultimate author and therefore gives it unity. As an evangelical and an exegete, I would argue vigorously for the validity of this principle. But again, the problem arises at the point of working it out in practice. The exegete, for example, is understandably concerned when he or she sees the imposition of a possible, but most highly improbable, meaning on a text in order to make it conform to other texts for the sake of unity, which is all too often the result of a prior commitment to the *shape* of that unity as much as to the unity itself. Unity is often understood to mean uniformity. That Scripture might reveal a diverse witness on some matters is ruled out before one even looks at the texts.

While it is certainly true that one can make a beautiful quilt out of whole cloth, it is also true that one can do so out of patchwork. Any two pieces of patchwork lying side by side in isolation could appear so discordant as to make the dogmatician anxious. But when those two become part of a whole, with pattern and design, the glory of the quilt's unity lies precisely in the patterns of diversity. What would seem to be incongruous is patchwork without overall pattern or design— a concern the dogmatician rightly addresses to the exegete.

IV. Closing Remarks

To conclude: To insist that the very nature of Scripture, as the evangelical understands it, has locked into it a degree of ambiguity, accommodation, and diversity causes some people to capitulate in despair—either toward the certainties of fundamentalism or the ambiguities of liberalism. I, for one, opt for what I call the radical middle. If God gave us his word this way, and I believe he did, then our task is to hold on to both realities—its eternality and historical particularity—with equal vigor. If we cannot always have absolute certainty as to meaning or application, we can certainly move toward a higher degree of common understanding.

As I see it, the way toward that higher level of commonality is still to be found at the crucial point of authorial intentionality, which by its very nature we would insist is also thereby the Holy Spirit's intentionality. This does not mean that all words have the same intent. There is a different intent to poetry and a sentence of divine law. But all human speech has intent; and if we are to hear God's word rightly for ourselves, we must begin with that original intent. If God did not speak timeless aphorisms, he did speak an eternal word. That word had specific intent in its historically particular moments. The task of exegete and theologian alike is to discover/hear that word in terms of God's original intent. I would argue that it is that same word with its same intent that should now address us in our own historical setting. Instead of seeing this as a debility, we should see it as the greater glory of Scripture and praise God for it. That he would speak so directly to *their* contexts is what gives us hope that he will always through that same word speak again and again—to ours and all of humankind's individual historical contexts.

3

NORMATIVENESS AND AUTHORIAL INTENT: A PROPOSAL REGARDING NEW TESTAMENT IMPERATIVES

I concluded the previous essay by noting the inherent hermeneutical tension created by the evangelical view of Scripture. Because Scripture is God's word, on the one hand, we inherently look for absolutes and certainty; but because it was given in historical particularity, on the other, God himself locked in a degree of ambiguity and accommodation, on neither of which matters do evangelicals fully agree. Despite some of the difficulties involved, and despite the fact that in many cases we fall far more short of certainty than some would like, it was nonetheless suggested that the way through for us lay in the crucial question of the author's intent. In this essay, and the next, I would like to pick up this question and suggest *why* this is the crucial matter for us, and at the same time especially wrestle with the area of hermeneutics where most tensions arise among evangelicals—the New Testament imperatives. Here is where we are divided; and the issue is rarely on the meaning of texts in their original contexts, but on the universality and normativeness of their application.

The purpose of this present essay, then, is threefold: (1) to make some preliminary observations about hermeneutics and normativeness; (2) to explore further the crucial question of authorial intent; and (3) to offer a proposal within that framework for the New Testament imperatives that sees them as part of the gospel, not some new form of law.

I. Toward a Common Understanding of "Hermeneutics" and Normativeness

In striving for greater hermeneutical precision, it seems imperative that we work toward a common understanding of the word "hermeneutics," especially as to how the concept of normativeness fits into that understanding. It seems to me that by the term hermeneutics we ordinarily are not referring primarily to the many and varied ways that Scripture, having power on its own, speaks directly into our own personal lives. Rather, we are concerned about Scripture as the basis for Christian theology and behavior, and for the application of Scripture that is at once both universal and timeless. That is, we are concerned about the meaning and application of biblical truth that should be the same and obligatory for all people at all times and in all circumstances. We are interested here in the universal applicability of the biblical text, not the individual encounter with it.

We instinctively recognize the validity of this assumption in the area of Christian theology per se. The basic theological truths of the unity of God, creation, the deity of Christ, Christ's death as effecting atonement, etc. are not negotiable—not at least to the evangelical. These are the essential and universally applicable truths of the Christian faith, without which the faith is something other than truly Christian. But when it comes to Christian behavior and personal piety evangelicals often display a different attitude toward Scripture, where it becomes a kind of quarry for principles—a rule book to live by—or an instant source of divine guidance for any and all aspects of life.

By this differentiation I do not mean to play down the devotional reading of Scripture. Nor do I demean those moments when quite apart from its original context or intent, the Holy Spirit has used the text of Scripture with great power to speak to our need or situation. In September 1988 we dedicated our Regent College facility that sits at the entrance to the University of British Columbia, on a choice corner lot that for years was simply overgrown with wild vegetation. At the dedication, which was held outside on our spacious park, our former colleague Dr. Klaus Bockmuehl read the Scripture from Solomon's prayer of dedication in 1 Kings 8. It is hard to describe the power of that moment. Here at the entrance on the campus of a great university a school had been erected to integrate faith and learning, to speak Christ to the secular campus. And none had striven and prayed more for that dream than Dr. Bockmuehl himself. Though the setting was quite different from where those words were originally spoken, here were the words of Scripture—without comment— being spoken again and by the Holy Spirit becoming a living and powerful word.

And who of us in times of difficulty and dryness has not read from the psalms or prophets and had their vivid images of God's watering the dry places for Israel become a means of watering our own arid places? Such experiences, I would argue, lie within the inherent power of Scripture. After all, the very fact that so much in Scripture comes by way of vivid images and metaphors opens up possibilities for hearing and being ministered to in ways quite beyond the original author's intent.

On the other hand, although we very well might share with others such wonderful encounters in God's living word, none of us would dare to believe that such moments are intended to be universally applicable to all other believers. It is the very personal nature of such moments that gives all of us latitude toward others to have their own such moments with God. But the things that divide us are not related to that use of Scripture. Rather, our differences result from all of us looking at the same texts, all with a similar view of Scripture as the word of God, yet either understanding the *original meaning* of the texts in different ways or having different views as to how they do or do not apply. Here, it seems to me, our hope for greater consistency and larger agreement lies still with the primary task of hermeneutics—the careful exegesis of texts, which has the *original intent of the text* as its *primary* goal. Let us turn once more, then, to the question of authorial intent.

II. The Question of Authorial Intent

The crucial nature of the question of intentionality was put on display a few years ago in its starkest form by the then U.S. presidential adviser, and later attorney general, Edwin Meese. Just before Christmas, 1983, he made national headlines by declaring that he had not seen "any authoritative figures that there are hungry children in America" and that people eat in soup kitchens because it's free, not because they can't pay for it. Such absurdities were properly castigated by the media, one of whom, given the appropriateness of the season, suggested a resemblance to Scrooge. In his defense Meese argued that the Bob Cratchits of Dickens' story were not in such dire straits—Cratchit did have a job after all, and they also had a home and food—and that Scrooge was not really such an evil fellow, but rather has been the victim of a bad press. I know some who saw that rejoinder as clever and as setting his opponents straight. As a matter of fact, of course, it was neither clever nor true, but a clear display of one's theology setting the agenda for the reading of a text—and in this case a rather demonic theology. Meese's travesty of Dickens' *Christmas Carol* was to turn it on its head, so that it became the 180 degree opposite of *Dickens'* intent in writing the story. One may disagree with Dickens if one wishes, but it is totally illegitimate to destroy an *author's* intentionality in such cavalier fashion.

    I have used this rather stark example in order to get the reader's attention, for one of the genuine difficulties of evangelical hermeneutics is our aptitude to do a similar thing to the biblical text, but not recognize ourselves as doing so.

    In the previous essay, I argued that the inadequacy of liberal hermeneutics lies first in the liberal view of Scripture—an emphasis on its being given in human words so that the divine word is either blunted or diminished—and second in the liberal view of religious authority, which rests ultimately on human reason. The net result is the autonomy, or idolatry, of the self. We tell God what is permissible in Scripture to be his word.

    Anyone hearing me say that and having a careful ear and an observant eye to the contemporary evangelical scene should have had his or her mental wheels turning. How different is that from an evangelical, who, by selective hermeneutics or with a theological a priori, manages to disregard or get around what is equally unpalatable in the text. Is there really much difference between a liberal, whose philosophical predispositions allow him or her a reinterpretation of the bodily resurrection of Jesus into a spiritual ideal of life after death, and an evangelical, whose political or economic presuppositions allow him or her to reinterpret, or disregard altogether, the biblical mandate of securing *mishpat* (justice) for the poor (that is, the oppressed and disenfranchised), which means *not* that they get what's coming to them but that they are to receive mercy? If the one abuses the intent of the text so as to frame a "modern" theology, the other abuses the intent of the text so as to secure his or her inalienable rights to affluence, materialism, and selfishness.

Unfortunately, it is the liberal who seems able to see this inconsistency in us better that we ourselves. This is surely one of the valid critiques in James Barr's rather scathing, if sometimes intemperate, denunciation of what he calls fundamentalism.[1] Because liberals tend to deny the *prior* authority of Scripture, it is easy for them to interpret texts as they will, as far as present or eternal relevance is concerned. But when liberals watch evangelicals vehemently attack them on crucial *theological* points, yet casually get around equally crucial *ethical* points, because evangelicals, too, seem to have made prior commitments as to what God may say to them, liberals are scarcely convinced that our view of Scripture is a helpful one. All the more so, when we leave the impression that because we believe God inspired the text, he must also be on our side in the interpretation of the text, even when we neglect or distort it to fit our prior commitments.

What shall we say, then? Do we capitulate, simply because our autonomy over the text takes place at a different point? Not at all, I would argue. The difficulty I have with liberal hermeneutics remains. I do not see any hope for a corrective to their autonomy over the text. They may be corrected by reasonable arguments, but reason still prevails, not the text of Scripture itself. What one doesn't like in Scripture, one may simply disregard or interpret to fit one's presuppositions.

But precisely because evangelical hermeneutics places the final authority in the text itself, there is always the

[1] James Barr, *Fundamentalism* (London: SCM, 1977). See, e.g., pp. 310–17.

hope that God the Holy Spirit will have his way and disabuse us of our prejudices and call us to obedience to God's will. Because the authority is intrinsic to Scripture itself, the evangelical, by theological predisposition, should always be open to reformation. Sadly, that does not happen nearly as often as it should because we also tend to have the theological disposition that our prior theological, ecclesiastical, and ethical commitments are correct and not in need of reformation, an issue I wish to address in a further essay.[2]

But it is this conviction of ours about the inherent authority lying in the text of Scripture that makes the issue of authorial intentionality so crucial. This is why we insist that good exegesis is *always* the first step to sound hermeneutics. And good exegesis is so only as it seeks to discover and hear what the text is *intending* to say.

The reason for such insistence on intentionality rests with the nature of spoken or written communication. Except for rare exceptions like E. E. Cummings, speakers or authors intend for their hearers/readers to understand what they are trying to communicate. Indeed, even Cummings has the intent of *no* intent in his poetry, so that too is not without intentionality.

There is, of course, a different intent, for example, to a psalm and a letter. The poetic nature of a psalm, which appeals to both mind and feeling, has inherent in it the possibility that one may hear more than the poet intended.[3] So also with the powerful, basically poetic, images of the prophets, who also set a further dimension of understanding into motion when they committed to writing what was originally a spoken word. Even so, the very *choice* of poem over straight prose has such further hearing as a part of its intent; but a poet

---

[2] [See chapter 5.]

[3] Precisely this failure to recognize the differences between types of discourse attenuates so much of the argument against intentionality by David C. Steinmetz ("The Superiority of Pre-Critical Exegesis," *Theology Today* 37 [1980] 27–38). This article has an unfortunately large number of failures of this kind, including the fact that by starting with Benjamin Jowett's insistence on "one meaning," he has set up something of a straw man with regard to contemporary hermeneutical discussion and thus fails to address much of the present discussion which is miles removed from Jowett.

surely hopes also that the reader will hear *the poet's* own joy or pain and understand *the poet's* allusions or images.

My point is a simple one. Since God chose to communicate himself to us through human speech in historically particular circumstances, we are locked into a hermeneutical process that demands by its very nature that we listen carefully first of all to what is intended; for there alone lies our hope of hearing what God himself wants us to hear.

By insisting on the priority of exegesis in the hermeneutical task, however, we are not thereby arguing for the autonomy of exegesis. In fact, to insist on authorial intentionality as the crucial issue does not presume to have made the hermeneutical task easier. Such an insistence has a twofold aim: (1) Authorial intentionality serves as a *corrective*, or sets some limits, as to what texts may *not* be made to mean. One need only think of how B. B. Warfield interpreted "the perfect" in 1 Cor 13:10 to refer to the canon of New Testament Scripture to recognize the cruciality of original intent. It must be a hermeneutical axiom for the straight prose of a letter that the "meaning" of the text cannot possibly be something neither the author nor his readers could have understood .[4]

(2) Authorial intent is also the way forward for us to construct our theologies in a truly biblical fashion. It will teach us that in theology not all apparently conflicting data need to be resolved or harmonized. Sometimes such data can stand side by side in healthy tension. That, too, is a form of unity and reveals the many-splendored glory of God. Furthermore, authorial intentionality should guide us through some of the more gray areas where we are divided as to the application of texts. I hope to illustrate this in some detail in the next chapter.

---

[4] Some have objected to this axiom as limiting the power of the Holy Spirit to give meaning to texts far beyond the mind or intent of the original author. But in this case Paul himself sets the limits. In 1 Cor 5:9 he is quite upset with the Corinthian congregation because they have either misunderstood or, more likely, disregarded his own intent in an earlier letter. For him there is only one meaning to his words—his meaning; and they are quite blameworthy for having disregarded it. People simply do not use the letter form if they expect people to find all kinds of deeper or hidden meanings in their words. There are other types of discourse for this purpose.

But to argue for the intentionality of texts as the *prior* hermeneutical task does not resolve all our difficulties. It is merely the way forward. Several hermeneutical tasks remain. My concern in the rest of this essay is to explore especially the way evangelicals tend to treat the biblical imperatives; and at the same time I am concerned to offer a different model for our consideration, one which attempts to be true both to the intent of the text of Scripture, on the one hand, and to the intent of the gospel itself, on the other.

III. A Gospel Framework for New Testament Imperatives

One of my basic concerns about evangelical hermeneutics in the past is our tendency to adopt a very cognitive, rationalistic model which often misses either the nature of the gospel itself or the dynamic quality of life in the Spirit—matters that are absolutely fundamental to the very Christian life that our hermeneutics is concerned about. This is especially true of the fundamentalist's use of texts, where Scripture very often becomes the quarry from which one mines propositions to be believed and imperatives to be obeyed. But the net result of such hermeneutics more often than not is that it turns both Scripture and the gospel into a form of Christian law, as devastating as the pharisaism which Jesus denounced or the Judaizers against whom Paul spoke so vehemently. Such hermeneutics sees Scripture as the divine *rule book;* in this hermeneutics three things tend to happen: (1) First there is a tendency to level all Scripture and thereby take all the imperatives across the board, thus mining the quarry and offering a new set of Christian rules to live by; the ad hoc nature of the texts is recognized only when what is mined does not fit theological predispositions (tongues, head-coverings, etc.).[5] (2) But secondly, fundamentalists accomplish this by frequently flawed exegesis and an especially selective hermeneu-

---

[5] [Typical of fundamentalists' hermeneutics was their reaction to men's "long hair" in the late 1960s—on the basis of 1 Cor 11:14. Without blinking, they made this incidental part of Paul's argument normative, while his main point, that women should have a head-covering when praying or prophesying, was considered ad hoc.]

tics, so that consistency is nearly impossible to come by. (One whole wing of evangelicalism, for example, argues vehemently for the eternal validity of 1 Cor 14:34–35 on the silence of women, while rejecting every other imperative in the chapter, including the final one, not to forbid speaking in tongues—all on the basis of a prior commitment to an exegesis and hermeneutical a priori that simply cannot be sustained in terms of author's intent.) (3) Once the new set of rules is in place, subscribers to this method use it as a measuring stick by which all deviant beliefs and behavior are judged and found wanting.

Missing in such hermeneutics is the dynamic of the gospel itself and especially of the Spirit. Here one is declared to be saved by faith, because that is clearly taught in Scripture; but in actuality one is finally related to God on the basis of works—in this case by means of close adherence to the rules of the faith as they have been worked out by a very rationalistic hermeneutics, where there are no uncertainties and where everything is neatly packaged. Furthermore, obedience tends to be quite non-relational. One obeys the rules as they are extracted from the book, and the rules tend to be very task- not people-oriented. To put all that more theologically, the call to obedience is to God, not the Bible; it is to a divine Person, not to a collection of written rules.

While it is easy for us to see fundamentalists behind the foregoing description, what concerns me is that "enlightened evangelicalism" at times tends to operate from a very similar hermeneutics. Perhaps the easiest place to see this in operation is in the question which I hope to address in the next chapter—the debate over women's ministries—where often with a kind of splendid casuistry that makes it look all very cogent, some women are excluded from their own calling to ministry because a single text is treated as law. Besides the fact that such a view misses the much greater amount of material on the other side of things and that it probably misses Paul's own ad hoc intent by a considerable margin, such a view seems to miss the redemption and freedom afforded by the gospel and to favor instead some alleged, divinely ordained hierarchical structures—which can only be found after, not before, the Fall. Insistence on head-coverings, or sabbath observance, or tithing all tend to follow the same hermeneutical procedure. Each in its own way misses the greater power of the gospel and the role of the Spirit in Christian ethical or religious life and turns biblical texts into rules for Christians to abide by. After all, in Pauline theology in particular, the primary imperative is, "Walk in/by the Spirit" (Gal 5:16)—all other imperatives flow out of that one.

Lest some get nervous for fear that I am putting the use of Scripture aside for something rather more subjective, I would argue that such is not so. To the contrary, I am urging two things: First, we simply must take more seriously than we do that there are *differences of degrees and levels in the New Testament imperatives.* Abstaining from sexual immorality or clothing oneself with compassion, humility, and forgiveness are of a different kind and of a different category from the guidelines for the exercise of prophecy and tongues in 1 Corinthians 14 or for the discipline of sinning elders in 1 Timothy 5. The very fact that Paul himself gives plainly different guidelines for the marriage of widows in 1 Corinthians 7 and 1 Timothy 5 should tell us something about the nature of these kinds of texts, as over against those that in some way or another are illustrations of the double love command—love for God and love for neighbor.[6]

Second, over against the fundamentalist hermeneutics of the New Testament imperatives, which many evangelicals have never quite freed themselves from—for fear of being seen to abandon Scripture itself, I would guess—I am urging something much closer to Jesus' own rejection of scribal models of interpretation in Matthew 5 in favor of a hermeneutics that is more biblically relational, based on the character of God and the gift of the Spirit. One does not get angry with a brother, not because the law forbids killing, but because in the kingdom of God we have become children of a heavenly Father who is not like that, and the very redemptive nature of the gospel makes *love* for neighbor one's first ethical priority. To make "no anger" a new law to replace "no killing" in the Ten Commandments is to miss too much. All things are now measured by the character of the Father; as his children we are privileged by the power of the Spirit to bear his likeness in the world. The ethical demands of Matthew 5, therefore, illustrate

[6] [I will pursue some of this in more detail in the next chapter.]

how such life is be lived out in a variety of settings—all relational. And in the kingdom of God, in Jesus' teaching, God's demand is always accompanied by his gift. Ethics is response to the experience of grace, as the story of Zacchaeus illustrates most profoundly.

So also with Paul's own rejection of circumcision and food laws. One is no better off or worse off doing either. Such religious duties simply do not count. Therefore, Paul neither urges that Jews stop circumcising their children nor allows that Gentiles must circumcise theirs. The freedom of the gospel, and life in the Spirit, eliminate such matters as *obligations;* but they do not eliminate or condemn those who are more comfortable with such practices than otherwise; hence with Jews Paul lives as a Jew. What is disallowed is for those who practice them to make them mandatory for those who do not.

The same is true with such a perfectly innocent matter as tithing. For all that one can say about its value and usefulness as a kind of minimum guideline for Christian giving, one quite misses the gospel when it is turned into some kind of Christian requirement. The gospel frees one from such a reading of biblical texts. But does it thereby also free one from giving? To the contrary, according to Paul, the gospel, with the gift of the Spirit, teaches one a kind of generosity that emulates the lavish gift of grace found in the one who "though he was rich, yet for our sakes became poor, that we might be made rich" (2 Cor 8:9).

What I am urging is not that we do our exegesis differently, nor that we get around texts that we don't like; rather, I am urging that we learn to think of biblical texts not as *rules to follow,* but as expressions and *illustrations of God's redemption,* and therefore as *guidelines for our living redemptively* in a fallen world.

IV. Application

Let me conclude, then, with two illustrations as to how such a model might work out in some very painful contemporary issues, on which we lack agreement, and which are so charged with emotion and personal pain that it is difficult for some even to engage in hermeneutical discussion about them—lest the issues be lifted from real life and be made the playground of theoretical ethics. I refer to the issue of abortion and the question of divorce and remarriage, and in both cases I am concerned not simply with how Christians themselves respond to these issues, but how they respond in a fallen world which for all practical purposes is trying to deal with moral issues quite apart from the reality of God. I turn to the first one, abortion, because Scripture does not speak directly to it, while in the other it does.

Let me say right up front about abortion that I am one of those who is convinced that as biblical Christians we must work to bring this horror to an end. But what concerns me is that I feel so little in common hermeneutically with other evangelicals who share my conviction. On the one hand, we must acknowledge that Scripture nowhere speaks directly to the issue. With others, I too believe that it is nonetheless covered by the sixth commandment—thou shalt not kill, in the sense of committing murder. But a hermeneutics that approaches this issue as obedience to law seems also to create people who very often break other expressions of the same law in their vehemence against those who do the abortions and those who have them done. In the name of Christ they act unlike Christ for the sake of their "Christian law."

But what shape might a redemptive hermeneutical model take? I would suggest that it begins biblically not with the law, but with God himself, whose character is revealed in the law, when it is viewed first as *gift* before obligation. God as Creator, as the life-giver, as the one who has bestowed upon his human creatures the inconceivable gift of joining with him in the creation of yet another human life that will bear God's image, as well as that of her or his parents—all of this should make abortion under *any* circumstances immoral, but on demand unthinkable. We are the children of the living God, our heavenly Abba, whose many-splendored creativity and whose care for the oppressed and disenfranchised is being defaced in every abortion. Surely God looks on with both horror and compassion. "But judgment is mine," says the Lord, "I will repay." I would argue, therefore, that our response to this evil should be many-sided, but always one which leaves judgment in God's hands while we show compassion to those who so cavalierly destroy human life that we are convinced is precious in the sight of him who gave it in the first place.

Perhaps we might begin with a day of mourning, in which we weep before God in sackcloth and ashes over a people who seem to have such a callous attitude toward human life. On the other side, all those who oppose abortion in our modern world in the name of Christ must also be ready to be first in line to offer care and love for unwed mothers, for unwanted babies, for siblings of aborted babies who so often suffer their own form of trauma over whether they were wanted, and for those mothers whose abortions create such dissonance in their own lives that they must go through years of therapy.

But whatever else, our response toward the unborn must not be turned into law in such a way that our rules are more important than the people we perceive as breaking them. After all, it is not some abstract rule or obligation that is being shunted aside; it is a rejection of God's own character as loving Creator, and a rejection of grace and redemptive love. Our ethics must likewise be creative expressions of redemptive love; otherwise the law becomes the important thing, and we carry on with strident voices damning the very people for whom Christ died.

When we turn to the issue of divorce and remarriage, we come to one that is of a considerably different kind, because here we *do* have texts that speak directly to the issue—and they seem uniformly against it. No matter how compassionate one might wish to be to those who have experienced this personal tragedy, and no matter how much we might yet have to learn about the meaning of these various texts in their original contexts, one can scarcely escape the biblical view, expressed especially by Jesus, that God is against divorce. As Jesus put it, God had something in mind from the beginning for our human race and for our basic relationships as male and female that stands over against divorce. Or to put it my way, with tongue in cheek, the reason Jesus said "no divorce" is that he also said "love your enemies."

As anyone who has tried to wrestle with this issue knows well enough, the hermeneutical complexities surrounding it are considerable—and that for several reasons, many of which have nothing to do with our own scene. (1) It is clear that the injunctions in both Jesus and Paul presuppose a believing community; and since Paul in particular distinguishes between how a believer and unbeliever respond on this matter, it seems clear that this is not an issue that can be legislated outside the Christian community. That is, those outside Christ are playing to a different set of rules on this one (although even in their case much can be said positively in favor of marital faithfulness). (2) It also seems to be the case that both Jesus and Paul were speaking into contexts where divorce was being advocated (or at least sanctioned) by members of the believing community. Indeed the Pharisees' view of divorce by the time of Jesus, in which they divorced in order to remarry and remarried in order to divorce, was simply "legalized caving in before the pressure of sexual passion."[7] And in the case of Paul it was the threat from a more ascetic ideal that he had to fight against. Thus they do not speak to the question of divorce in general, nor to situations where there have been desertions or wife abuse. (3) Even so, it is clear that they expect people within the believing community not only not to pursue divorce, but in the case of Paul to live with their spouses in loving and self-giving ways that are determined by their relationship to Christ.

Our problems stem from a whole variety of forces: (1) the general self-centeredness of our culture has made its way into the church as well; (2) the amount of wife abuse is staggering in our culture—and this even within Christian homes; (3) people come from so many kinds of dysfunctional family backgrounds that stable family life is often foreign to them, so that they bring all the wrong kinds of models to the marriage relationship.

In light of all this, what then serves as our hermeneutical model of gospel and Spirit rather than law? It seems to me that the way forward is to stay close to Jesus' and Paul's intent—that divorce sought after by believers should be discouraged in every possible way. But not because this is law, but because sought divorce as an excuse to remarry is simply pagan and reflects little or no understanding of the gospel at all, and as the way out of a difficult situation lacks the larger sense of the redemptive nature of the gospel that sometimes calls for suffering and hardship on our part. Christian men and women are first of all brothers and sisters in Christ before they

---

[7] This is the language of David L. Dungan, *The Sayings of Jesus in the Churches of Paul* (Philadelphia: Fortress, 1971) 121.

are husbands and wives, and that determines everything for them. They are to treat marriage partners with the kind of love that is required of all relationships within the believing community.

On the other hand, precisely because this is not law, and because many of our contexts differ so radically from theirs, our attitude should probably not be to save every marriage at all costs, but to seek a resolution in some cases on the basis of what is the most redemptive thing to do. Indeed, this it would seem to me is the ultimate question in all tough decisions about the New Testament imperatives, where we are seeking to reflect the gospel and life in the Spirit. What is redemptive? Since the paradigm of our faith is the cross, we should encourage some to seek for God's redeeming their failures. The model of our faith, after all, is not perfect people, but redeemed people, who have experienced grace and restoration.

V. Conclusion

I would thus urge that evangelical hermeneutics in the years ahead must increasingly think of Scripture less as law to be obeyed and more as gospel to be proclaimed, as redemption and freedom in Christ, as life in the Spirit, against which there is no law. And I would further urge that our hermeneutics in the years ahead must also find ways of penetrating our increasingly secular culture with the real gospel and its message of redemption. We must find ways of bringing back awe and mystery into a fictionalized, trivialized, and technological world—made the more so as we move closer and closer to a generation that knows nothing about life without television; once children had to learn creativity since they could not be babysat or mesmerized by an idiot box. All of these and more must affect the way we think about and apply Scripture in our hermeneutical future.

As our former student put it, "the ministry is hermeneutics." I would change that slightly, "Christian life is hermeneutics": it involves the hard but joyous work of listening yet more carefully and applying God's word to all of life in a fallen world.

4

THE GREAT WATERSHED— INTENTIONALITY AND PARTICULARITY/ETERNALITY: 1 TIMOTHY 2:8–15 AS A TEST CASE[1]

In the preceding two chapters it has been argued (1) that evangelical hermeneutics has as its primary task the need to hear God's word within the human words of Scripture, neither diminishing it as an eternal word, as liberal hermeneutics so often does, nor enshrining all the particulars, as fundamentalism so often does—but in inconsistent and frequently cavalier ways; (2) that the way forward still lies with the question of authorial intent; to discover *what* the human author meant by his words, and *why*, is at the same time to hear God's eternal word; and (3) that a hermeneutics of the New Testament imperatives should have a reflection of the gospel as its aim rather than a law code.

In this essay I want to return to the matter of imperatives and author's intent, and I will do so by raising one of the more difficult of our hermeneutical problems—created by the distancing factors of time and culture noted in chapter 2. The question is: Since God spoke his word in historically particular circumstances, *how much* of the *particularity itself* is a part of

---

[1] The substance of much of this chapter was first presented at the Evangelical Women's Caucus, Wellesley, Mass., June 1983.

the *eternal word*? For example, if we agree that the texts call us to practice hospitality, must we wash feet as a way of showing such hospitality? Is the particular (washing feet) the only—or necessary—way in which one is obedient to the eternal (showing hospitality)? If we agree (and not all do, despite 1 Corinthians 11:5) that women may pray and prophesy, must they do so with heads covered in order to keep male and female distinctions intact?

Let it be noted at the outset that we come now to one of the truly ticklish issues for evangelical hermeneutics. Indeed, some would reject the very way I have phrased the question, and in particular how I have phrased the two examples. Nonetheless, I am convinced that all evangelicals make this distinction in some way or another—although they rarely, if ever, articulate it—and that the lack of articulation on this matter is a major reason both for many hermeneutical inconsistencies and for many of the behavioral legalisms that abound among us.

To get at this question, therefore, what I call the great watershed, I propose to speak once more to one of the thorniest of our contemporary issues and to use it as a case study for several of the hermeneutical suggestions that were put forward in the previous essay. The issue: the role of women in ministry in light of Paul's intent in 1 Timothy 2:8–15.

The hermeneutics of liberalism has basically dismissed this text as irrelevant for today, usually on the grounds of a canon within the canon, in which allegedly deuteropauline texts reflect an early degeneracy from Paul's more open stance.[2] Among evangelicals the issue has been over cultural relativity. Some argue for the absolute normativeness of 1 Timothy 2:11–12—in all cultures at all times—on the grounds of a so-called creation order, based on vv. 13–14.[3] Other evangelicals, on the other hand, argue from the apparently culturally relative mat-

---

[2] See, e.g., Robin Scroggs, "Paul and the Eschatological Women," *JAAR* 40 (1972) 283–303. The term "liberalism" is not intended to be pejorative, but is used to distinguish a certain stance with regard to Scripture, as presented in chapter 2.

[3] See, e.g., D. J. Moo, "I Timothy 2:11–15: Meaning and Significance," *TrinJ* 1 (1980) 62–83; J. B. Hurley, *Man and Woman in Biblical Perspective* (Grand Rapids: Zondervan, 1981) 195–221; and scores of others in a variety of forms.

ters about dress in vv. 9–10, plus the fact of women's ministries found elsewhere in the New Testament, that vv. 11–12, though certainly intended to be binding on the local situation to which they were addressed, were not intended to be normative for the church throughout its history.[4] The anxiety most frequently expressed about this position arises from what is suspected to be hermeneutical arbitrariness or relativism. Who determines what is culturally relative if the text does not so express itself? And if this is culturally relative, then why not prohibitions against sexual immorality, or idolatry, or hatred, as well?[5]

I. The Historical Setting of 1 Timothy 2:8–15

Let us begin with an exegetical overview of our text, beginning at step 1—the occasion and purpose of 1 Timothy. Since my exegetical stance as to the purpose of 1 Timothy is spelled out in detail in the introduction to my commentary on this letter,[6] let me here simply outline the conclusions of that argument, without all the supporting evidence.

In contrast to an older view, which treated 1 Timothy as a kind of "church manual," I have argued that the key to understanding the letter lies in taking seriously that Paul's *stated* reason in 1:3 for leaving Timothy in Ephesus is the *real* one; namely, that he has been left there to combat some false teachers, whose asceticism and speculative nonsense based on the law are engendering strife, causing many to capitulate to the false teaching.

---

[4] See inter alia, D. M. Scholer, "Women's Adornment. Some Historical and Hermeneutical Observations on the New Testament Passages," *Daughters of Sarah* 6 (1980) 3–6; Fee and Stuart, *How to Read,* 66–69.

[5] See esp. the various anxieties raised by J. R. McQuilkin, "Problems of Normativeness in Scripture: Cultural Versus Permanent," in *Hermeneutics, Inerrancy and the Bible. Papers from ICBI Summit II* (ed. E. D. Radmacher and R. D. Preus; Grand Rapids: Zondervan, 1984) 219–40; and G. W. Knight, "A Response to Problems of Normativeness in Scripture: Cultural Versus Permanent," ibid., 243–53.

[6] In the New International Biblical Commentary series (Peabody, Mass.: Hendrickson, 1988) 1–31.

The key to identifying these false teachers is to be found in Acts 20:17–35, where in an address to the *elders* of this church Paul prophesies in v. 30 that from among *their own number* will arise those who will lead the church astray. This probability is supported by several data in the letter itself:

The fact is that the false teachers in this case are clearly insiders, not outsiders as elsewhere. Since teaching is the one clearly expressed duty of the elders (3:3; 5:17), it follows naturally that the false teachers were already teachers, thus elders, who have gone astray.

It seems certain from 2:9–15, 5:11–15, and 2 Timothy 3:6–7 that these straying elders have had considerable influence among some women, especially some younger widows, who according to 2 Timothy 3:6–7 have opened their homes to these teachings, and according to 1 Timothy 5:13 have themselves become propagators of the new teachings.

Several pieces of evidence suggest that corporate life in the church in Ephesus was experienced not in a large Sunday gathering in a single sanctuary, but in many house-churches, each with its own elder(s). The issue, therefore, was not so much that a large gathered assembly was being split down the middle, as that various house-churches were capitulating almost altogether to a leadership that had gone astray. Some new ideas that had been circulating just a few years earlier in Colossae and Laodicea had made their way to Ephesus, but now as the "official" line being promulgated by some of its elders. They must be stopped, and Timothy was left in Ephesus to do it.

The *purpose* of 1 Timothy, then, arises out of these complexities. The letter betrays evidence everywhere that it was intended ultimately for the church itself, not just for Timothy. But because of defections in the leadership, Paul does not, as before, write directly to the church, but to the church through Timothy. The reason for going this route would have been twofold: (1) to *encourage Timothy himself* to carry out this most difficult task of stopping the erring elders, who were creating strife as well as promoting errors; and (2) to *authorize Timothy before the church* to carry out his task. At the same time, of course, the church will be having the false teachers/teachings exposed before them, plus Paul's instructions to Timothy about what he was to do.

II. The Argument of 1 Timothy 2:8–15

In order to see the place and meaning of 2:8–15 in the letter, it might be helpful to review the overall scheme of the argument as it relates to this view of its occasion and purpose.

The letter itself is all business, lacking both the standard thanksgiving and concluding greetings. Instead, it both begins and ends with a charge to Timothy (1:3–7; 6:20–21), urging upon him the task of stopping the false teachers and counteracting their teaching. The opening charge (vv. 3–11) is basically a spelling out of the error of the false teachers, which is then, in a somewhat digressive way (vv. 12–17), contrasted with the gospel—in the form of personal testimony. This digression in turn is followed in vv. 18–20 by a resumption and repetition of the charge to Timothy.[7]

Chapters 2 and 3, then, joined to the charge by a "therefore,"[8] serve to give Timothy guidelines for restoring proper behavior to the church(es), both in their times of worship and in the appointment of new leaders. The concern in each instance has to do with conduct in the community, vis-à-vis the false teachers.

Chapter 4 then elaborates in some detail upon the two matters expressed in the charge in chapter 1: (a) the nature of the errors of the false teachers, insisting on their demonic origins (4:1–5), and (b) Timothy's role in Ephesus (4:6–16). Finally, Paul moves on to give instructions about how Timothy is to deal with the two specific groups who are the problem element—some young widows (5:3–16) and their "captors," the straying elders (5:17–25). This in turn is followed by a concluding indictment of the false teachers (6:3–10) and a final appeal to Timothy (6:11–16, 20–21). Thus the whole letter

---

[7] The resumptive nature of these verses, picking up the argument from v. 7, is made clear by the language (*parangeilēs*, 1:3; *parangelias*, 1:5; *parangelian*, 1:18), which is unfortunately glossed over in most English translations (the RSV being a happy exception).

[8] It is also commonplace both in translations (e.g., NAB, JB, Moffatt) and commentaries (e.g., Barrett, Hanson, Hendriksen, Moellering, Scott) to slide past this *oun* ("therefore") as though it were not there. But that will scarcely do, since *oun* appears regularly in Paul to press home an exhortation on the basis of what precedes (see e.g., Rom 12:1; 1 Cor 4:16; Eph 4:1).

deals basically with the false teachers and Timothy's role in Ephesus to stop their activity.[9]

First Timothy 2:8–15 is the second paragraph in the section on conduct in the community at worship, which is concerned first, in 2:1–7, with the proper *objects of* prayer—*all people,* because God wants *all people* to be saved as is evidenced by Christ's having given himself to redeem *all people.* Almost certainly this paragraph stands over against the elitism/exclusivism of the "new doctrines."

Then in vv. 8–15 Paul moves to proper *demeanor in* prayer. The men (v. 8) are to pray without getting involved in the quarrels and disputes engendered by the false teaching. The women likewise are to deport themselves in a manner befitting godly women. But the section about women receives a considerable elaboration, which is of high interest, both because it is so much longer than that of the men (cf. also 5:3–16 and 17–25) and because the final resolution is so clearly like that given for the young widows in 5:11–15. The paragraph is in four parts, each closely interrelated to what has gone before. In vv. 9–10 the concern is with dress; vv. 11–12 argue for a quiet and submissive spirit. In vv. 13–14 the modest dress and quiet demeanor are supported by illustrations from Genesis 2 and 3, while v. 15 sums up the whole by arguing that women's salvation lies in their accepting the role of mother, provided of course that they are truly women of faith, love, and holiness.

In vv. 11–12 she is also forbidden to teach and domineer a man, but it is clear from the whole paragraph, first, that this is only *part* of the problem—and not necessarily the most significant part—and, second, that the greater concern is for her to take her standard place in society, and thus in the church, as befits a woman who professes religion.

What is striking about this paragraph is its several points of correspondence with 5:11–15. First, it should be noted that in chapter 2, vv. 9–10 and 11–12 go together as two sides of one coin. There is an abundance of texts in antiquity that suggest that "dressing up" and insubordination on the

---

[9] See the radically different, and generally unsupported, overview of 1 Timothy given by Hurley, *Man and Woman,* 195–97, and notice how it affects his entire hermeneutical endeavor.

part of women, and especially wives, go hand in hand.[10] It is therefore not clear here whether the chief concern is with the women acting as women who are bent on seduction (vv. 9–10) or with their insubordination (vv. 11–12). In either case, they are "playing loose" with the norms of society, which is exactly what Paul says of the younger widows in 5:11–15. Rather than displaying the "good works" of the older widows, which includes rearing children well (5:10), they have apparently "given themselves to pleasure" (v. 6), have grown wanton against Christ in their desire to remarry (v. 12; apparently outside the faith). Furthermore, they have become busybodies, going about from house to house (house-church to house-church?) talking foolishness[11] and speaking of things they should not (v. 13; the false teachings? cf. the description of the false teachers in 1:6–7). As such they have already gone astray after Satan (v. 15). Paul's solution here is for them to remarry (vis-à-vis the false teachers; cf. 4:3) and bear children, so as not to give the enemy cause to reproach the gospel (v. 14).

The concern and solution in 2:9–15 are nearly identical. Instead of living for pleasure and becoming wanton against Christ, they should dress modestly and do good works (vv. 9–10, cf. the older widows). Instead of being busybodies and going about from house to house speaking foolishness and talking about matters that are none of their business, they are forbidden to teach, but rather are to learn in all quietness.

The point of vv. 13–14, therefore, is not primarily with the illustration from Genesis 2, about Adam's having been formed first—although that is clearly there and is not to be dismissed. What needs to be noted is that Paul does not elaborate that first point. He merely states it; its application can only be inferred. The second point, however, from Genesis 3, seems to be his real concern, since it receives an elaboration and leads directly to the conclusion in v. 15. Based on words of Eve in Genesis 3:13 ("the serpent *deceived* me, and I ate"),

---

[10] See Scholer, "Women's Adornment," and Fee, *1 and 2 Timothy*, 39.

[11] There is no known instance in Greek where the word *phylaroi* means "gossips." In fact it means to talk foolishness and is often used in contemporary philosophical texts to refer to "foolishness" that is contrary to "truth."

Paul states that Adam was *not* deceived (by the snake, that is), but rather it was the woman (note the change from Eve to "the woman"), who, having been deceived (by Satan is implied) fell into transgression.[12] That is exactly the point of 5:15—such deception of woman by "Satan" has already been repeated in the church in Ephesus. *But,* Paul says in v. 15,[13] there is still hope. She can be saved (eschatological salvation is ultimately in view, but in the context she shall be saved from her deception with its ultimate transgressions), provided she is first of all a woman of faith, love, and holiness.

This, then, is the point of the whole—to rescue these women and the church from the clutches of the false teachers. Their rescue includes proper demeanor in dress, proper demeanor in the assembly (including learning in all quietness), and getting married and bearing children (one of the good works urged in v. 10, seen in light of 5:9–10).

III. Application and Historical Particularity in 1 Timothy 2:8–15

That leads us finally to ask the ultimate hermeneutical question, How does it apply? which in light of our original question may now be put something like this: Given the ad hoc nature of 1 and 2 Timothy, with their own specific historical particulars, how do the instructions given by Paul to *that* historical situation function as an eternal word in the church for all times and climes? Or, to put that in another way, in hearing that word in our day, how much of the *original historical particulars* is *also* part of the eternal word to our lives?

The problem here is exacerbated in part by our own inconsistencies. For example a considerable literature has emerged over verses 11–12, pro and con, as to whether women may teach, preach, or be ordained; but there is not a single piece that argues from 5:3–16 that the church should care for

[12] It is absolutely foreign to the text and to Paul's argument to suggest, as does Moo, that women by nature are more susceptible to deceit and "that this susceptibility . . . bars them from engaging in public teaching" (p. 70 [see n. 3]).

[13] A clearly adversative *de* that begins this clause is omitted in most English translations. The contrast is to the "woman falling into transgression; *but* she shall be saved. . . ."

its widows over sixty or require the younger ones to be married. One can understand the reasons for this, of course; our agendas have been set by our own cultural or existential urgencies. But the inconsistency is there; to get those who are doing battle over 2:11–12 to own up to it is extremely difficult.

I would propose here that at least a part of the solution toward greater consistency lies with authorial intentionality. What did Paul himself intend by these instructions? Would he have considered them *all* applicable to all believers at all times? In answer to that question, I suggest that a variety of *kinds* of statements are made in his letters, with *differing kinds of particularity and intentionality.*

Let me illustrate—and do so by starting with an extreme end, so as to clarify my point. In 2 Timothy 4:13 Paul, sitting in a Roman prison and asking Timothy to come before winter, tells him (by way of imperative) to bring the cloak he had left in Troas with Carpus. How many of us have ever tried to obey that text? And why not? Because common sense tells us that *all* of it was for Timothy and therefore was not meant for our obedience. In this case the statement is so ad hoc that it had *no intent* of any kind beyond the personal concern to stay warm next winter.

But let's take another text—from the same letter. In 2:3, in equally ad hoc circumstances, Paul tells Timothy to take his share of suffering as a good soldier of Christ Jesus. This one, we instinctively sense, could well apply to us. For good reason. For although Paul had no one else but Timothy in mind when he dictated those words, lying behind this personal injunction is a considerable appeal to Christian discipleship, based on Christ's and Paul's example (1:8–14), that we ourselves recognize as moving beyond that historical particular to all who would be disciples of Christ.

So also with all the second person plural ethical imperatives to the communities in Paul's letters. We sense that they are intended to transcend the particulars.

We, too, should be forgiving, walk in love, be full of compassion, do all things without grumbling and complaining. I would argue that an inherent universality is latent *in Paul's own intent.*

That brings us to the more difficult texts: those that lie somewhere in between. Here consistency is hard to achieve, because eternality in terms of the particulars is not at all clear. It is at this point that I would place 1 Timothy 2:11–12, where Paul enjoins that the women in that context are to learn in a quiet demeanor; they are not to teach or domineer a man. And I want to make sure that we look at such a text in conjunction with its companion texts, vv. 9–10 and 15, which equally enjoin that women are not to dress expensively, to plait their hair, or wear pearls, and that their salvation lies in bearing children. Moreover, we must also bring into the discussion the companion texts in 5:3–16 that widows over sixty, who are known for good works, who have no family, and who have not remarried, are to be supported by the church, while the younger widows are required to remarry, bear children, and keep house.

Let us begin with 5:3–16, because so few of us bring that to the twentieth century. Indeed, for most of us it's a matter of, Who cares? The reason for this is quite simple. Even though we still have widows, in most cases in our culture they have a considerably different status, and thus it is simply not an issue for most of us. Besides, we let the state handle these matters for us. *Here we have clearly let changes in culture determine how we particularize for ourselves their historical particulars.* We simply do not think that widows under sixty are disobedient to God if they do not remarry. In any case, we have some ambiguities here, since in 1 Corinthians 7:39–40 Paul *dis*courages such remarriages.

So also with 2:9–10 and 15. We relegate those texts to cultural changes, and rightly so. We still need to hear the word about modesty and appropriateness of dress, but on the specifics most evangelicals have long ago yielded to cultural change. Almost certainly Paul himself did not intend these instructions to address all Christians in all churches universally. All of these instructions, including 2:11–12, were ad hoc responses to the waywardness of the young widows in Ephesus who had already gone astray after Satan and were disrupting the church.

It simply cannot be demonstrated that Paul *intended* 1 Timothy 2:11–12 as a rule in all churches at all times. In fact the occasion and purpose of 1 Timothy as a whole, and these verses in particular, suggest otherwise. Nor will it do to appeal to vv. 13–14 as though there were some eternal order in creation, since *neither* Genesis *nor* Paul makes that point. After all, in Romans 5:12ff., in a quite different context where Christ serves as the representative *man* whose death and resurrection is for all (male and female), Paul argues considerably differently about the origin of sin in the human race. In that context Adam, not Eve, is seen as the origin of sin—precisely because Adam was a *man*, and thus the representative man whose sin led all (male and female) into sin.

I would argue, therefore, that the answer to our hermeneutical question lies in the area of our obedience to the ultimate concern of the text, even if at times the particulars are not carried over to the "letter." This is how *all* of us treat 1 Timothy 6:1–2 (about slaves and masters)—although such was not always the case. This is probably how many would argue that they are obeying 5:3–16—although I for one would like to probe about a bit more here. Why not, then, with 2:11–12, since *all* do it with the preceding vv. 9–10?

Such a hermeneutical stance makes some people nervous. They see this as hermeneutical arbitrariness or relativism, a kind of capitulation to culture that causes us to go contrary to God's word. That this is indeed a somewhat culturally conditioned response I would not deny, just as our response to 5:3–16 is equally culturally conditioned. That in itself is not a bad thing, given the very ad hoc nature of Scripture that demands we regularly hear the word anew in our own contexts. But that it is a capitulation and that it leads to disobedience, I do deny. To the contrary, such a view seems further supported by several other hermeneutical considerations put forward in the two preceding essays.

First, here is a clear case where, just as with the remarriage of widows, there is a diversity of witness within the New Testament itself. Most who oppose women in ministry recognize this, but have argued either (a) that this is a didactic text, while all others are descriptive, or (b) that this text at least prohibits women to teach when adult males are present, although other ministries such as prophecy are open to them,[14]

---

[14] See, e.g., Wayne Grudem, *The Gift of Prophecy in the New Testament and Today* (Westchester, Ill.: Crossway, 1988), a popularized and expanded version of the author's published Ph.D. dissertation, *The Gift of Prophecy in 1 Corinthians* (Washington: University Press of

or (c) that this prohibits any form of "ruling leadership" (including ordination), although other ministries are available.[15] The problem with these solutions, however, is that they are not only casuistic—some of them would do the Pharisees proud—but that they seem to turn the New Testament evidence on its head.

For example, it is especially difficult to see how, in the New Testament, teaching is a more authoritative ministry than prophecy or evangelism—especially in light of 1 Corinthians 12:28 (*second* prophets; *third* teachers), or how teaching in this passage involves "ruling leadership" or "ordination." Moreover, it is in fact the *only* certain text of its kind in the New Testament;[16] whereas, the rest of the New Testament evidence indicates that women had a considerable role in ministry and leadership in the early church—especially so in light of both Jewish and Greco-Roman culture.

My point is a simple one. It is hard to deny that *this* text prohibits women teaching men in the Ephesian church; but it is the unique text in the New Testament, and as we have seen,

---

America, 1982). This position is based on a series of unverifiable arguments, which in turn function as assumptions, to the effect that (a) OT prophecy was primarily an authoritative, revelatory function; (b) in the NT apostles function as the OT prophets; therefore (c) NT prophecy is a different thing altogether; (d) since teachers are also authoritative persons, women may prophesy, but not teach, since (e) despite what Paul actually says, teaching is a more authoritative gift than prophecy. Much of this argumentation is simply specious and has little to do with the concerns of Paul in his letters.

[15] I had this argument presented to me by two different scholars from the Reformed tradition in two different public debates at Gordon-Conwell Theological Seminary. In both cases I found it quite impossible to get past the hurdle of presbyterial church order, which they simply assumed as the biblical one and insisted must be in view in this passage. Despite what the text actually says, one was quite insistent that "some sort of juridical authority must be in view here." The issue thus turned out to have little to do with the function of teaching as such, but with the role of women in the governmental structures of the church, which seems to be a reading of the text on the basis not of Paul's own concerns but of one's own theological urgencies. [See chapter 5.]

[16] Since 1 Cor 14:34–35 is almost certainly a textual corruption, as I have argued in my commentary (NIC on 1 Corinthians, Eerdmans, 1987).

its reason for being is *not* to correct the rest of the New Testament, but to correct a very ad hoc problem in Ephesus.

Second, I would like to pursue further one of the hermeneutical models for the future that I proposed in the previous chapter. The concern has to do with our tendency to turn the gospel into law, or canon law, that essentially rejects the freedom and redemption of the gospel itself. There are several factors involved here. One is our tendency to miss the profoundly Spirit-centered nature of New Testament ethics, so that God's righteous requirements are written on our hearts by the Spirit, and we thus live and walk in the Spirit. Paul says that for such ethics there is no law. This does not mean freedom to do anything one wishes; rather, it means freedom to live out the gospel redemptively and relationally in a fallen world. In such an ethics obedience is not to rules and regulations, but to God himself, who has both created us and gifted us richly to serve him by serving one another.

The second factor is closely related: It is to argue that such a hermeneutical paradigm calls us to see the redemption of the cross as its primary pattern and focal point. In our present case, it is to argue that the atonement of Christ has overturned all the effects of the Fall, including the blighting curse on both men and women pronounced in Genesis 3. This does not mean a denying of male and female distinctiveness— that is a part of creation and the image of God—but it does mean a restoration of their lost joint mandate both to image God (now in a fallen world) and to serve together in having dominion over the earth. It is hard to imagine under any circumstances how the denial of one half the human race to minister to the other half brings glory to the gospel, which intends to break down such barriers and bring redemption to the whole body.

The third—and related—factor is the clincher for me: To deny women to minister and teach in the church is to deny the clear gifts of God himself. Here we would do well to learn from Peter in Acts 10–11, when the Holy Spirit did the unthinkable thing of falling on Gentiles who were uncircumcised, and say to the religious, "Who was I that I could withstand God?" If God had never gifted a woman to teach, then of course one might have a case—but such a person would also be living in a radically different culture from ours—or with his or her head in the sand.

IV. Conclusion

In conclusion, I realize, of course, that not all will be satisfied with this articulation. But one must allow that it comes from a New Testament scholar who is also a believer, and whose great passion is the gospel and our own response of obedience. For those who disagree, may I kindly urge that they articulate their own hermeneutical model, but let it be a model that reflects redemption, not law.

And in any case, in all that we do, let us talk to one another—and fervently love one another.

5

HERMENEUTICS, EXEGESIS, AND THE ROLE OF TRADITION[1]

In the course of these essays, although not always articulated as such, I have merely noted—and passed over—the role of tradition in the whole hermeneutical enterprise. That matter I now wish to pursue in some detail. My concern has to do with how our various presuppositions, especially ecclesiastical and theological presuppositions, affect the exegetical and hermeneutical enterprise, both positively and negatively. Since all hermeneutics is done within a circle, or circles, of tradition, the burden of this essay as an "issue in evangelical hermeneutics" is for evangelicals to learn a more discriminating recognition and articulation of the role of tradition in our hermeneutics.[2]

[1] I am grateful to several members of the biblical and theological faculties of the Canadian Theological Seminary and Canadian Bible College for taking time to interact with this essay in its lecture form, and to Peter Davids for sending me a synopsis of that interaction, which allowed me further to clarify my thinking at several points.
[2] For a penetrating essay on some aspects of this question, see J. Ramsey Michaels, "Scripture, Tradition, and Biblical Scholarship," *The Reformed Journal* 20 (May-June, 1970) 14–17.

I. On Defining "Tradition"

I begin with some definitions, since for the New Testament scholar "tradition" can mean any number of things, and in this essay certainly will. "Tradition" tends to have five distinct nuances, which can be illustrated in the following nearly impossible sentence: The New Testament documents record the tradition(1) of Christ and the apostles, which early church tradition(2) understood to be inspired and authoritative Scripture; the later church codified tradition(3) so that it became equally authoritative with Scripture, an understanding which those within the evangelical tradition(4) reject, but who nonetheless frequently interpret Scripture through the lenses of their own personal and theological traditions(5). Thus:

Tradition to the New Testament scholar ordinarily refers to the oral and early written stage of the New Testament materials. This includes Christ's proclamation of the kingdom of God, the apostolic proclamation of the gospel, and the teaching that surrounded and followed its proclamation that was "handed down"[3] by the apostles to their converts. In this sense the New Testament itself is a written representation of that tradition, which the church came to understand as the inspired and authoritative expression of what is essential for Christian faith. Although the most common use of the term for the New Testament scholar, this one will not be addressed in this essay.

For the later church, tradition described the reflective understanding of things Christian, expressed in the consensus of the teachers of the church. What most evangelicals tend conveniently to ignore is that it was tradition in this sense that was responsible, under the guidance of the Spirit, for the canonization of the tradition in its first sense. It should also be noted that in the early going this "body of understanding," although authoritative, was not official and was itself in process of formulation. Such matters as canon, Trinity, church order, and infant baptism belong to tradition in this sense, where the seeds of understanding lie within the New Testament, but their explication belongs to a later time. Obviously,

---

[3] The English word "tradition" derives from the Latin equivalent of the Greek word *paradidōmi*, which means to "hand down."

on some of these matters we are more agreed than on others, which is one of the difficulties for us—namely, the interplay between the New Testament documents themselves and their explication in the early church.

In time tradition in the second sense developed into its third sense, found especially within the Roman Catholic communion, where church tradition holds an official and authoritative role in the church's life, equal to Scripture itself. This, of course, is a primary area of self-conscious difference between evangelicals and Roman Catholics, and probably why evangelicals historically have been uneasy about tradition in the second sense.

This in turn leads to the fourth sense of the term. From at least the time of the Great Schism of 1054, and especially since the Reformation, the bifurcation of the church into its many streams caused each of these streams—and rivulets, if you will—to develop its own tradition. Hence there is the evangelical tradition, the Pentecostal tradition, the Baptist tradition, etc. Although often unofficial, tradition in this sense is quite often as powerful a force among evangelicals as it is among Roman Catholics. Here is one of the clear curses of the Protestant penchant for sectarianism, where the role of tradition is to protect vested interests in the things that "make us differ."

Finally, there is a non-technical nuance to tradition, which refers to that entire set of experiences and settings making up one's personal history, that one brings to the biblical text before ever a page is opened. For believers that includes one's own personal experiences, sociology, culture, family and religious/ecclesiastical histories, and national history. The problems emerge when these traditions are not recognized as such and therefore often intrude upon or impede the exegetical and hermeneutical enterprise.

My concern in this paper is to reflect on the way that tradition in senses 2, 4, and 5 impacts evangelical hermeneutics. My primary concern is with senses 4 and 5, although a few probings with regard to the second sense are also offered. In none of these three senses, of course, are we talking about bad things, but about necessary and inevitable things. On the one hand, one simply cannot, or at least should not, interpret biblical texts as if there were no tradition in the second sense.

In both the Pentecostal and evangelical traditions to which I belong, there is no recognition of an official tradition as speaking for the whole church in the third sense, but neither are we willing to jettison the whole Christian tradition in the second sense. Hermeneutics, we would argue, must be a community affair; and the first community to which we are debtors is that of the church in history.

On the other hand, neither can one escape the impact of tradition in the fourth and fifth senses. Indeed, much of our difficulty lies here. First, there is that kind of unofficial—often unwritten and therefore sometimes more powerful—ecclesiastical or theological tradition to which we belong, to which we have varying degrees of commitment; and as members of this tradition we often feel compelled to defend it or to speak prophetically to it. Wittingly or unwittingly, this tradition shapes both our approach to and our understanding of the biblical texts.[4] But this is but one part of a larger whole. Second, there is the additional factor of living within a certain cultural, historical, and sociological milieu that impacts so much of how we think or perceive things. This too impacts our understanding.

The difficulties here are twofold: On the one hand, tradition in the fifth sense is so much a part of one's own presuppositional history that often we rather automatically assume our traditions are the shared experiential history of everyone else. On the other hand, there are times when one is more consciously aware of one's tradition, and then tries to make the biblical evidence read in support of that tradition.[5] In this latter case one moves toward a kind of hearing and reading of texts that would seem to get in the way of the text, not letting the text have its own impact on one's theology and experience.

[4] In fact it was pointed out by one of the faculty at Canadian Theological Seminary that my own predominant wrestling with the Pauline imperatives in these essays probably reflects something of my own set of traditions as New Testament scholar and churchman.
[5] This is one area, it should be noted, where the biblical scholar within any given tradition (in the fourth sense) often lives in conflict within that tradition, because he or she is so often prone to reexamine the tradition on the basis of the biblical texts, rather than the other way about.

My interests in the rest of the essay are three: My primary concern is to illustrate the several ways—innocently, subtly, or more consciously—the fourth and fifth senses do in fact affect our hermeneutics, sometimes quite adversely. Secondly, and briefly, I want to urge that the effect of tradition on hermeneutics in itself is not necessarily a bad thing. Finally, I would like to offer some preliminary suggestions for finding a way forward so that tradition may be fully affirmed and appreciated, on the one hand, but not allowed totally to skew our hermeneutics, on the other.

II. Presuppositions and the Exegetical–Hermeneutical Endeavor

In a now famous essay, Rudolf Bultmann once asked whether it was possible to do presuppositionless exegesis, in answer to which he gave a resounding No.[6] We bring too much of ourselves—our culture and our traditions—to make such exegesis possible. Although he was contending in particular against a sterile historical positivism, his essay continues to be a byword in biblical studies.

If that is true for the more purely historical task of exegesis, how much more do our presuppositions play a key role in the larger hermeneutical endeavor of theological relevance and application. It is simply not possible for us *not* to bring our own experience of faith and church to the biblical texts. The very *selectivity* of our hermeneutics, illustrated in the preceding chapter with regard to women teaching and widows remarrying, is for the most part related to our traditions, not to our exegesis. Our difficulties here can best be demonstrated by illustration rather than argumentation.[7]

Let me begin at the more innocent level, where experiential, cultural, or ecclesiastical assumptions are simply read into the text without thought or recognition. It may take

[6] "Is Exegesis Without Presuppositions Possible?" in *Existence and Faith, Shorter Writings of Rudolf Bultmann* (Cleveland: Meridian Books, 1960) 289–96.
[7] I am fully aware of my own vulnerability in what follows, as I hope eventually to make plain. As any perceptive reader will recognize, the very choice of illustrations, and the selective nature of them, says something about my own "tradition" in the sense that I have just defined it.

such simple forms as when someone from my part of the country reads Psalm 125:2, "as the mountains are round about Jerusalem," and thinks *real* mountains rather than the flat, elevated plain that surrounds the low promontory between two wadis on which ancient Jerusalem sat; or when hearing of "building one's house on sand" one thinks of long sandy ocean beaches rather than the chalk valleys of the wadis scattered throughout Judea. Or it may take a more churchly form, where one presupposes one's own experience of church (whether building or liturgy), when one reads the texts that speak of the gathered church or of sitting at the Lord's Supper. What, for example, could possibly be further from the New Testament experience of the Lord's Supper than an individual cup and wafer, passed along the pew where people sit facing other people's backs, and tacked onto the end of a preaching service, or of going forward to an altar (!) to be administered wafer and cup by a priest?

But it can take more subtle forms as well. Take, for example, the Pentecostal doctrine of the baptism of the Holy Spirit, as subsequent to and distinct from conversion and evidenced by speaking in tongues.[8] In all fairness to Pentecostals, much of this understanding came about through a very common approach to Scripture, where Scripture is understood to be establishing historical precedent, and therefore a necessary experience, for subsequent believers. Moreover, the original outpouring of the Spirit at the turn of this century came as a direct result of some students in Topeka, Kansas, who were diligently seeking Scripture for the secret to the empowering of the early church. I have elsewhere addressed the question as to whether precedent may be rightly used to establish normative Christian practice;[9] but it should be noted

[8] [For a more detailed analysis of the hermeneutics of this issue see chapter 7.]
[9] See chapter 6 in *How to Read*, 87–102. Cf. chapter 6 below, where in an earlier version of this same concern directed toward Pentecostalism in particular, I have tried to put this matter on somewhat firmer hermeneutical ground. It should be noted that James R. Goff, Jr., challenges the notion that the doctrine of initial evidence derived from community exegesis. In his book, *Fields White Unto Harvest: Charles F. Parham and the Missionary Origins of Pentecostalism* (Fayetteville: University of Arkansas, 1988), Goff suggests that Parham had specu-

that the concept of "subsequent to and distinct from," which forms part of Pentecostal theology at this point, came less from the study of Acts, as from their own personal histories, in which it happened to *them* in this way, and therefore was assumed to be the norm even in the New Testament.

Such subtlety with regard to one's tradition may take a more sophisticated posture in the form of New Testament scholarship itself. I think, for example, of how two great scholars like Archibald Robertson and Alfred Plummer so cavalierly treat Paul's Greek in 1 Corinthians 11:10 ("For this reason a woman ought to have authority on her head"). Convinced that the passage is dealing with the subordination of women—despite the fact that this sentence says something quite the opposite—they comment: "That 'authority' is put for 'sign of authority' is not difficult; but why does St. Paul say 'authority' when he means 'subjection'?" Mind-boggling, to say the least. Or take their comment at the outset of chapters 12–14, "The phenomena which are described, or sometimes only alluded to, were to a large extent abnormal and transitory."[10] Transitory, in terms of subsequent historical development, yes; but abnormal, hardly. Careful exegesis of all the texts demonstrates that in the Pauline churches at least, these were the normal patterns of Christian experience. But how else could two Anglicans at the turn of the twentieth century have understood these texts? They simply lacked the ecclesiastical or experiential frame of reference for Paul's own experience of the Spirit and church.

In a similar vein, one is reminded of how the leading lexicographer in the history of New Testament scholarship, Walter Bauer, treated the name of Junia in Romans 16:7. His own experience of church simply disallowed that Paul could include a woman under the title of "apostle," so the entire entry is devoted to trying to justify reading the name as Junias (a man's name), even though there is not a shred of evidence for such a name in the Roman world.

lated as early as 1899 that tongues (for Parham, xenoglossa, speaking in a foreign language) was the spiritual key to world evangelization in the last days (pp. 69–76).
[10] *A Critical and Exegetical Commentary on the First Epistle of St Paul to the Corinthians* (ICC; Edinburgh: T & T Clark, 1911) 232, 257.

But equally as often, the impact of tradition in its various forms is far less innocent, and indeed may be judged to be rather conscious, and sometimes pernicious. Take, for example, that unfortunate book sent out free to almost all North American clergy a few years back, Robert Schuller's *Self-Esteem: The New Reformation.*[11] Here is a case in which culture not only determines how one reads texts, but does so at the expense of the clear meaning of the texts themselves.

The heart of Schuller's "new reformation" is a redefinition of human fallenness in terms of romantic humanism. The basic human problem is not that people are fallen, living in rebellion, pride, and disobedience, but that they lack self-esteem. "The core of sin," Schuller says, "is a negative self-image," and rebellion is only one of its external manifestations (pp. 66–67). I would dare say that no two people in two billion could read Genesis 3, or Psalms 32 or 51, or Romans 1–3 and derive that view of the human condition. The problem here is not simply letting culture get in the way of one or a few texts, but of the *whole* of Scripture. Schuller's view stands in basic contradiction to biblical revelation.

When he comes to his supporting texts for finding self-esteem as the way forward, the restructuring of meaning is even worse. Schuller begins, one should note, by asserting that "sacred Scriptures are our infallible rule for faith and practice" (p. 45); he then goes on to assert, rightly I would argue, the priority of the Lordship of Christ. But in Schuller's hands this becomes a ploy to bypass original intent altogether in order to use the Lord's Prayer as Christ's own commission to encourage people to be done with the "six basic, negative emotions that infect and affect our self-worth" (p. 48). What follows is an interpretation of the Lord's Prayer with an occasional moment of validity but which overall is so far removed from Jesus' own intentionality that he would scarcely recognize it. Gone is its eschatological framework of the already/not yet of God's rule, gone its theocentric opening petitions, gone its humbling of the one praying before the mercy and grace of a loving Father. In its place stands a God who is all soft mush and prayer that calls people to self-dignity, to a noble self-love, to

[11] Waco, Tex.: Word Books, 1982.

become "sincere, self-affirmed, divine-adventurers, striving to succeed" (p. 50).

What is simultaneously so subtle and devastating about this is that it is cloaked with evangelical buzz-words, and assumes an evangelical posture toward Scripture. But here indeed is hermeneutics gone astray, where tradition in the form of one's culture has the final word, and God's strong and powerful word is blunted at best, and misdirected altogether at worst.

But if this example is somewhat less helpful, because for most of us the flaw is so easy to spot, it may serve its purpose as a more extreme example so as to help us to see where other forms of tradition, especially ecclesiastical and theological tradition, may have equal capacity to "do in" the word of God.

I think, for example, of how so many in the Reformed or Dispensational traditions argue vigorously about 1 Corinthians 14:34–35 (that women are to keep silent in the churches) that this is an eternal word for the church in all places at all times (suspect as that text is as to its authenticity[12])—yet they reject everything else in chapter 14 as not permissible for today, despite the clear imperative in vv. 39–40 *not* to forbid speaking in tongues. Only prior commitments to one's tradition could possibly allow for such hermeneutical inconsistency. The greater problem, of course, is that they are quite convinced that there is no inconsistency at all. No wonder those standing on the outside of a given tradition looking in wonder whether there is any hope for an evangelical hermeneutics at all.

Similarly, I recall a debate that I was involved in with three other scholars at Gordon-Conwell several years ago, over the issue of women in ministry, including church structures. I had come from a tradition in which that had been my experience from my youth up. Precisely because of this, I indicated that it never occurred to us in our tradition to read 1 Timothy 2:11–12 or 1 Corinthians 14:34–35 except as ad hoc words to the local situations. God the Holy Spirit had preceded our looking at the texts by gifting women equally with men, so we asked, as Peter at Cornelius' household, "Who are we that we can withstand God?"

[12] On this issue see my commentary on 1 Corinthians (NIC; Grand Rapids: Eerdmans, 1987) 699–708.

It turned out that that admission on my part damned everything else I had to say. My views of 1 Timothy were obviously based on experience, not on exegesis. But what amazed me is that the scholar who made this charge assumed his own presbyterial church order not only to be *biblical*, but the *only* biblical model; and he simply could not be convinced that it was his own experience of church in which women did *not* speak, which had equally conditioned everything he had to say when he addressed the Timothy text. Indeed, at one point in a question-and-answer time, when quizzed about this matter, he blurted out, "Well, there must be *some* kind of juridical authority in the text!" To myself I thought, only a Presbyterian could have read the text in such a way (!); and he could not bring himself to see how much his tradition was affecting everything he said about it.

I have had similar interest in reading the reviews of my recent commentary on 1 Corinthians, which turned out to be generally positive. But in those parts where even favorable reviews must offer words of caution to their readers, the two places where I have been challenged most frequently are on some observations I make about church order in 1 Corinthians, or lack thereof, and about the charismatic phenomena. It will surprise no one that the reviewers who have taken exception to the matters on church order are Anglicans and Lutherans, while Dispensationalists to a reviewer bemoaned my handling of chapters 12–14. "But alas," one of them wrote, "Dr. Fee is also a Pentecostal." And then he went on to point out all the things wrong with my point of view, none of which, interestingly enough, were exegetical points, and all of which were based on his prior, unquestioning commitment to his own hermeneutical tradition.

There is one further way in which a prior commitment to tradition affects our hermeneutics, perhaps the most subtle of all, and therefore the most difficult for all of us to overcome. It has to do with how tradition (usually in the form of a prior theological system) leads us to ask questions of the text in the first place, which then tends to lead us to the kinds of hermeneutical posture we are predisposed toward.

Here let me illustrate from a book basically known only within a given tradition, which is by and large intended to reassure those within that tradition that those outside have an inadequate hermeneutics. The book in mind is by Professor Richard Gaffin of Westminster Seminary, entitled *Perspectives on Pentecost*.[13] The basic problem I have with Gaffin's book, and the reason for its inclusion here, is his subtle use of the analogy of Scripture,[14] which is both predisposed toward a given theological system and intermixed with skillful theological logic and the exegesis of texts so as to arrive at a predetermined conclusion. In the process, in texts he otherwise exegetes rather carefully, Gaffin tends over and again to disregard Paul's own ad hoc intentionality in favor of making them speak to questions that are not only not inherent in the texts and contexts themselves, but in fact are finally quite in opposition to the texts and their contexts.

Gaffin has approached his concern by addressing a series of narrowing concentric circles, always moving toward the singular question of the cessation of the gifts of prophecy and tongues. When he gets near to the inner circle of questions, the argument has the following steps:

(1) Prophecy and tongues function similarly, both being what he terms "*revelatory* gifts."[15]

(2) On the basis of Ephesians 2:20 he argues that apostolicity and prophecy are also to be understood as "*foundational* gifts."

(3) Since apostles ceased after their function of being "foundational" for the church, so too did the prophets [although this seems to fly full in the face of actual church history].

(4) Since tongues and prophecy function alike (from this view), then tongues, too, should cease with the apostles and prophets.

(5) Finally, he argues that it is gratuitous to assume that 1 Corinthians 13:10 intends that tongues should continue

---

[13] Philadelphia: Presbyterian and Reformed, 1979.
[14] [On this matter in evangelical hermeneutics, see chapter 2, pp. 34–35.]
[15] This in itself is a thoroughly unsupportable position. It is clear from 1 Corinthians that the "revelation" involved in prophetic utterances is in no way similar to the kind of revelation found in Scripture itself. Such prophecies are both ad hoc and need to be "weighed" or "discerned" by others.

until the Eschaton, and with further circles of logic he tries to discount that assumption.

What makes this argument persuasive to some is its apparent logic, coupled with the author's obvious ability to exegete individual texts. However, quite apart from some highly questionable exegesis of the key texts in 1 Corinthians, for which space does not permit a rebuttal here, what I find particularly not persuasive is the fact that the logic *precedes* the exegesis. Indeed, the whole enterprise has its logical form structured by asking a question to which not one of the biblical texts intends an answer. Gaffin's overruling question is, *When* will tongues cease? The one text that addresses that question at all—and even there it is quite incidental to Paul's real point—is 1 Corinthians 13:10, which almost certainly intends, "at the Eschaton," as its answer.[16] But since that answer is the one Gaffin is uncomfortable with, he sets up his logical circles to answer his own question with, "at the end of the first century." But in no case does he, nor can he, show that the answer to *that* question is a part of the biblical author's intent in the texts that are examined. He circumvents that by suggesting that it was the *divine* author's intent, on the basis of his own form of "analogy of Scripture."

I would contend that this is not a legitimate use of the analogy of Scripture—because the question is a wrong one. Indeed, what should be noted here is that traditional Pentecostalism has had its own way of posing questions and arriving at answers, albeit with much less exegetical sophistication. Their question is: Should all speak with tongues when baptized with the Spirit? Their answer of course is Yes. But that is determined *not* on the meaning and intent of the biblical texts themselves, but by the very framing of the question in that way.

Let me finally conclude this critique of others, with the candid admission that I do not with all of these illustrations suggest that I come to the text with a clean slate. I give them in part to illustrate what a tenuous task this is; in fact, knowing a bit about the basic sociology of the first-century believers and their thought world, I often wonder whether it is possible for the average North American, white, Protestant to understand

---

[16] On this matter, see my commentary.

the Bible at all, since such people assume their own middle class sociology to be that of the New Testament, whereas almost exactly the opposite is the case. But I am also illustrating in part how much easier it is to see this problem in others than in oneself. And that is precisely the great hermeneutical danger—that the biases of others are so clear!

III. Handling Traditions

Having set the reader up with all of this, let me now seem to reverse myself and say that coming to the text with our tradition(s) in hand is not in itself a bad thing. Indeed, it is impossible to do otherwise. But what I want to stress here is that in itself this is neither good nor bad, and that in fact, it may often serve to the good. Some years ago, when Samuel Beckett's play *Waiting for Godot* first appeared on Broadway, it had only limited success and soon left. But some months later it played at San Quentin, where it was an immediate and thoroughgoing hit; the inmates applauded and applauded— not because they were being given a bit of culture, but because they identified so thoroughly with Estrogen and Vladimir, who simply waited for Godot, who never came.

That experience brought it back to Broadway, where it had a long run and huge success. The "tradition" of the inmates at San Quentin gave them an understanding that allowed others to see it through different eyes—much closer to Beckett's, I would guess.

Thus it often happens that our own tradition(s) cause(s) us to read a text in a certain way and to assume it to be the only way, or the right way. And then someone with a different tradition reads and interprets the text, and suddenly something like scales fall from our eyes. Take, for one example, what I consider to be one of the significant contributions of the peace churches to the rest of us—to help us read the texts from the perspective of the early church on matters of peace and war, and not to assume that "my country right or wrong" was in fact something said by Paul or John—or could possibly be a Christian understanding of nation.

I think in this regard of my own experience of celebrating the baptism of thirty-seven new converts—all men— in rural Senegal some years ago. It was rainy season, so there was a large watering hole just away from the huts of the village where the baptism was to take place. After a "brief" service (one hour at 135 degrees Fahrenheit) in their newly constructed "church building," we paraded through the village to the watering hole for the baptisms. Of course, for such a new event the entire village turned out. What struck me was the outburst of laughter when, after his confession of faith in the Lord Jesus, the first of the new believers was immersed. They had never seen such a thing—and a religious ceremony at that! But as I watched the others, one by one, declare his own faith in Christ before the laughing—and sometimes mocking—crowd, I suddenly had a strong sense that all other baptisms that I had experienced were much less like the New Testament experience than these. I have never again easily read past the texts that say, "and they were all baptized." In the New Testament baptism was a public event, not cloistered in a church in the presence of only believers.

There are scores of other illustrations; I offer these simply to say that tradition per se is not the problem. To the contrary, the ability to hear texts through the ears of other traditions may serve as one of the best exegetical or hermeneutical correctives we can bring to the task.

Let me add also that if the ability to transcend one's tradition is rare, it can be and has been done—and often enough that we are usually in great debt to those who so do. For example, it was such insights by Hermann Gunkel on the Spirit in the New Testament,[17] and by Johannes Weiss on the place of apocalyptic in the New Testament,[18] which stood over against the entire stream of late nineteenth-century New Testament scholarship with its non-personal approach to the Spirit and its "soft mush" Jesus, that first really allowed the first-century documents to be true to themselves on these matters. Of course, as one reads Gunkel or Weiss one picks up a strongly iconoclastic bent to them, which thus sets in

---

[17] *Die Wirkungen des heiligen Geistes nach der populären Anschauung der apostolischen Zeit und nach der Lehre des Apostels Paulus* (Göttingen: Vandenhoeck & Ruprecht, 1888).
[18] *Die Predigt Jesu vom Reiche Gottes* (Göttingen: Vandenhoeck & Ruprecht, 1892; 2nd ed. 1900); Eng. trans. of 1st ed., *Jesus' Proclamation of the Kingdom of God* (Philadelphia: Fortress, 1971).

motion a *new* set of presuppositions. But at least they caused the whole world of Germanic scholarship to stop looking at the texts with the presuppositions of nineteenth-century idealism. And there have been other such moments, where whole new possibilities of hearing the ancient texts on their own terms have been made more available to us. So all is not lost.

But even more importantly, let me now return to the role of tradition in the second sense noted earlier. Here I begin with an observation, that is also a plea. By and large, evangelicals need to take more seriously the word of 2 Peter 1:20, that "no prophecy of Scripture is a matter of one's own interpretation" (NRSV). Exegesis and hermeneutics, even when worked on or worked out in the privacy of one's own study, must finally be the product of the Christian community at large. At this point, we all stand indebted to that long history of orthodox consensus. If, for example, on the doctrine of the Trinity church tradition has been far more positive about what certain texts taught than the exegete might be comfortable with, such tradition was never far afield in terms of what was inherently embedded in the New Testament texts, even if not precisely or intentionally explicated.

In scores of other areas, tradition, the reflective understanding of the biblical texts in the church throughout its history, has forged out for the church the theological undergirding for its various structures and practices; and even when it has needed to be corrected, or has been judged and found wanting, this is not the work of one or a few. To put it baldly, where there is no appreciation for tradition, for the rich heritage of reflective theologizing with its general consensus on the basic Christian verities, Protestantism has spawned a mass of individual heresies, all vying for center stage as the single truth of God.

IV. Conclusion

That leads me finally to say a few words as to how we might trace our paths through this most difficult of tasks, to be simultaneously both affirming and critical of our tradition(s) in the exegetical-hermeneutical endeavor. Here I have only some reflections and observations, nothing definitive:

With regard to the tradition of the church (in the second sense), it very well may be that we could learn to recognize levels of tradition, which might be given different weight.[19] For example, some issues have been heavily reflected on as central issues of the faith, and the church has come to a high level of consensus concerning them, a consensus that has held for centuries and that is common to the Eastern church, the Western church and the mainstream of Protestantism. Moreover, such understanding seems to be quite the point, or at least in keeping with the thrust of, the biblical texts themselves (e.g., the Trinity; the Person of Christ).

Other doctrines, on the other hand, have not been the focus of much theological reflection, even though they have assumed positions with a high level of consensus for centuries. Here one might think of the traditional role of male leadership, with the general failure to recognize the giftedness of women, or when recognized, to allow such gifts to operate only within the confines of women with other women.

At yet another level is the interpretation of single verses or passages, which have virtually never been the focus of church reflection. For this reason, there has often been a variety of interpretations of certain texts, with no sense of reflective consensus as to their meaning. Here the ongoing work of exegesis is itself a part of the formulation of the tradition.

If evangelicals are to take tradition more seriously as to its role in the hermeneutical process, a weighing of tradition in this manner might be useful. It would take a lot of evidence for one cautiously to disagree with the first level of consensus, whereas one might do so more easily at the next levels. In any case, such an understanding of tradition might help us to take it more seriously, without giving it absolute authority.

With regard to the effect of tradition in the fourth and fifth sense, the first and most difficult task is for any one of us to be able to discover our own traditions, and how in many different ways they affect our exegesis and hermeneutics. Here the only secret is no secret at all; it requires the effort of a lifetime—to be vigorously demanding of oneself, so as to spot when it is our biases that are at work or when we are more truly listening to God's very word for ourselves and for others. I

[19] For the substance of this paragraph I am especially indebted to the faculty interaction from Canadian Theological Seminary.

think, for example, of such a simple thing as the recognition of our own personal histories in a thoroughly individualistic culture, and how differently—and more correctly—we will understand and apply texts when we recognize the essentially corporate—people as a whole people—presupposition that lies behind all the epistolary imperatives. Think, for example, how differently one understands 1 Corinthians 3:16–17 or Philippians 2:12–13, when one thinks not in terms of individual obedience to such texts, but of their corporate nature—calling a community to obedience in terms of its new self-understanding in Christ.

Or I think further of the whole, generally rationalistic, and almost totally *literary* (= written) culture in which the North American inerrancy debate has taken place—without once recognizing how different a basically *oral* culture handles such things as precision in wording or in the transmission of traditions. This is not to discount the concern that brought about that debate, but it is to question whether much of it would have had meaning to the earliest Christians, whom we encounter in the pages of the New Testament itself.

Third, and of equal—or perhaps greater—significance, is a willingness on the part of all of us to be open to one another—to reexamine how we perceive our tradition as affecting us, especially in light of how others perceive it. This, of course, can be terribly threatening, because most of us take considerable comfort—and rightly so—in the stability and security that tradition affords. There can be little question that we are emotionally so constructed that we can handle the examination at the perimeter with much greater detachment than an examination of the core.

The final suggestion is the most difficult of all to put into practice, and that, of course, is that we actually change— or be willing to change or modify—rather than become more defensive. It may well be, of course, that such examination will lead to a greater confidence in the basic correctness, or value, of one's own traditions. But may God the Holy Spirit give us integrity and readiness to change or modify, if that seems to be needed.

6

HERMENEUTICS AND HISTORICAL PRECEDENT—A MAJOR ISSUE IN PENTECOSTAL HERMENEUTICS

Walter J. Hollenweger offers this interesting dedication to his comprehensive survey of Pentecostalism in the churches: "To my friends and teachers in the Pentecostal Movement who taught me to love the Bible and to my teachers and friends in the Presbyterian Church who taught me to understand it."[1] This statement by a former Pentecostal reflects the strength of Pentecostalism in general and its weakness in hermeneutics in particular.

Pentecostals, in spite of some of their excesses, are frequently praised for recapturing for the church its joyful radiance, missionary enthusiasm, and life in the Spirit. But they are at the same time noted for bad hermeneutics. Thus, in the more recent irenic treatments of Pentecostals and their theology—such as those by James D. G. Dunn,[2] Frederick D. Bruner,[3] Hollenweger,[4] and Clark H. Pinnock[5]—one finds words

---

[1] *The Pentecostals. The Charismatic Movement in the Churches* (Peabody, Mass.: Hendrickson [reprint], 1988) xvi.
[2] *Baptism in the Holy Spirit* (SBT 2/15; London: SCM, 1970).
[3] *A Theology of the Holy Spirit. The Pentecostal Experience and the New Testament Witness* (Grand Rapids: Eerdmans, 1970).
[4] See Hollenweger, *The Pentecostals.*
[5] With Grant R. Osborne, "A Truce Proposal for the Tongues Controversy," *Christianity Today* 16 (Oct. 8, 1971) 6–9. See also Pin-

of appreciation for the Pentecostal contribution alongside a critical assessment of the exegetical base for its distinctive teaching on Holy Spirit baptism.

I. The Problem

Although other exegetical and theological problems are sometimes noted, the crucial issue for Pentecostals in hermeneutics lies at their very heart, namely, with their "distinctives": (1) the doctrine of subsequence, i.e., that there is for Christians a baptism in the Spirit distinct from and subsequent to the experience of salvation, a doctrine which Pentecostals share with many "non-tongues" expressions of Christianity, and (2) the doctrine of tongues as the initial physical evidence of baptism in the Spirit.

An example of the formulation of these distinctives may be found in articles 7 and 8 of the "Statement of Fundamental Truths" of the General Council of the Assemblies of God:

> 7. The Baptism of the Holy Ghost
>
> All believers are entitled to and should ardently expect and earnestly seek the promise of the Father, the baptism in the Holy Ghost and fire, according to the command of our Lord Jesus Christ. This was the normal experience of all in the early Christian Church. . . . This experience is distinct from and subsequent to the experience of the new birth (Acts 8:12–17; 10:44–46; 11:14–16; 15:7–9). . . .
>
> 8. The Evidence of the Baptism in the Holy Ghost
>
> The baptism of believers in the Holy Ghost is witnessed by the initial physical sign of speaking with other tongues as the Spirit of God gives them utterance (Acts 2:4). The speaking in tongues in this instance is the same in essence as the gift of tongues (1 Cor 12:4–10, 28), but different in purpose and use.[6]

It will be noted that the sole biblical support for these teachings consists of passages from the book of Acts. It is important to note further that in the literature of the move-

---

nock's essay in *Perspectives on the New Pentecostalism* (ed. R. P. Spittler; Baker, 1976) 182–92.

[6] *Minutes of the Thirty-fifth General Council of the Assemblies of God* (Miami Beach, Fla., August 12–16, 1973) 102.

ment the experience of the apostles in Acts 2:4 is often seen as subsequent to their "conversion" experiences in John 20:22. One also finds the doctrine of subsequence supported by the example of Jesus, who was conceived of the Holy Spirit, but endued with power by the Spirit at his baptism.[7] Thus for Pentecostals the baptism in the Holy Spirit subsequent to conversion and evidenced by tongues is "the clear teaching of Scripture," based on biblical historical precedence. The Acts of the Apostles is the normative record of the normative primitive church. Therefore, the apostolic experience is the normative model for all Christians.[8]

Those who disagree with Pentecostals on these points usually argue in two closely related veins. First, they argue that one must distinguish between *didactic* and *historical* portions of Scripture, and that for the formulation of Christian doctrine and experience one must go primarily to the didactic portions, and only secondarily to the historical.[9] Secondly, what is *descriptive history* of the primitive church must not be translated into *normative experience* for the ongoing church. Pinnock and Osborne have put these two arguments together thus: "Didactic portions of Scripture must have precedence over historical passages in establishing doctrine," and " . . . the book of Acts does not establish a normative experience for the believer today."[10]

II. Some Preliminary Observations

Two observations should be made about hermeneutics within the traditional Pentecostal movement. First, their

---

[7] See esp. Ralph M. Riggs, *The Spirit Himself* (Springfield Mo.: Gospel Publishing House, 1949) 47–61; cf. Dennis and Rita Bennett, *The Holy Spirit and You* (Plainfield, N.J.: Logos International, 1971) 23–25.

[8] Hollenweger, *The Pentecostals*, 321, cites a Swiss Pentecostal confessional statement which says: "The apostolic church is its obligatory model." [This understanding of "normative" = "obligatory," and therefore a matter of obedience or disobedience has controlled all my discussions on this matter. See the "postscript" in section VI below for a further discussion of this matter.]

[9] See, for example, John R. W. Stott, *The Baptism and Fullness of the Holy Spirit* (Downers Grove Ill.: Inter-Varsity, 1964) 8, and Anthony Hoekema, *Holy Spirit Baptism* (Grand Rapids: Eerdmans, 1972) 23–24.

[10] "A Truce Proposal," 8.

attitude toward Scripture regularly has included a general disregard for scientific exegesis and carefully thought-out hermeneutics. In fact, hermeneutics has simply not been a Pentecostal thing. Scripture is the word of God and is to be obeyed. In place of scientific hermeneutics there developed a kind of pragmatic hermeneutics—obey what should be taken literally; spiritualize, allegorize, or devotionalize the rest. Pentecostals, of course, are not alone in this. Furthermore, gifted people tend to apply this hermeneutic with inspired common sense. Therefore, although aberrations abound in Pentecostal pulpits and sometimes in their pamphlets, the mainstream of traditional American Pentecostalism has treated Scripture in very much the same way as have other forms of American fundamentalism or evangelicalism. The differences have been over what is to be literally obeyed.

Secondly, it is probably fair—and important—to note that in general the Pentecostals' experience has preceded their hermeneutics. In a sense, the Pentecostal tends to exegete his or her experience. For example, the doctrine of Spirit-baptism as distinct from and subsequent to conversion did not flow naturally out of the Pentecostal's reading of Scripture. What happened was that they had themselves spent considerable time after their conversion sensing a lack of spiritual power. They saw the dynamic, life-transforming quality of the apostolic experience in Acts 2 and asked God for something similar. When they did have a dynamic experience in the Holy Spirit, they said with Peter, "This is that." That it happened after their conversion helped them to see this very pattern in Scripture: they saw the analogy with Jesus and the apostles, and the precedent in Samaria (Acts 8) and Paul (Acts 9). What followed was perfectly natural. They took the scriptural pattern they had found, supported by their own personal experience and that of thousands of others, and made it normative for all Christians.[11]

[11] [It has been suggested that this paragraph is not quite accurate historically, and that the earliest Pentecostals became so from their searching of the Scriptures. I acknowledge this bit of history in chapter 5, pp. 71–72, n. 9. But my point still remains. It was not a natural reading of texts that led them to a view of distinct from and subsequent to. They were in search of something, and found it. This is

William Menzies has suggested, rightly I think, that my statement needs to be qualified in a slightly different way, namely, that the Pentecostals did not look to the text for the *origination* of a theology, but for the biblical/theological *verification* of their experience (see "The Methodology of Pentecostal Theology: An Essay on Hermeneutics," in *Essays on Apostolic Themes: Studies in Honor of Howard M. Ervin* [ed. P. Elbert; Peabody, Mass.: Hendrickson, 1985] 13).

In defense of Pentecostals, it should be observed that although they have tended to arrive at the biblical norm by way of experience, they are not alone in establishing norms on the basis of historical precedent rather than on the explicit teaching of Scripture. The practice of infant baptism and the theology of its necessity are based first of all on the exegesis of some historical passages in Acts and one in 1 Corinthians (7:14); they are made normative on the basis of the historical precedent.[12] (Roman Catholic theologians would prefer the word "tradition.") The Baptists' insistence on baptism by immersion is based on no clear statement of Scripture, but rather on the exegesis of certain passages (including word study: "to baptize" = "to immerse") and historical precedent.[13] The partaking of the Lord's Supper every Sunday is required by some Christians on the basis of historical precedent (Acts 20:7).[14] Likewise, on the basis of Acts 2:44–45 some groups in

not quite the same thing as simply reading texts and coming to the conclusion that it clearly teaches that this is the norm of Christian experience.]

[12] See especially the debate between Joachim Jeremias and Kurt Aland: Jeremias, *Infant Baptism in the First Four Centuries* (Philadelphia: Westminster, 1960) and *The Origins of Infant Baptism* (London: SCM, 1963); Aland, *Did the Early Church Baptize Infants?* (London: SCM, 1961); Pierre Ch. Marcel in *The Biblical Doctrine of Infant Baptism* (London: James Clarke, 1953) bases his argument on the related hermeneutical principle of the analogy of faith.

[13] It is interesting to see the Bennetts assume a moderate stance on this issue of historical precedent: "It is assumed that you who are reading this book and who accept Christ will receive or have received baptism in water in the manner of the particular Christian fellowship to which you belong, and in accordance with your understanding of what the Scripture teaches about it" (*The Holy Spirit and You*, 25–26).

[14] It is of interest that the Assemblies of God sees baptism by immersion as "commanded in the Scriptures," but makes no state-

the Jesus-movement required the selling of possessions and having all things in common. Even such fringe groups as the snake-handlers argue for their distinctive practices partly on the basis of historical precedent (Acts 28:3–6).

The hermeneutical problem, therefore, is not unique to Pentecostals. It has to do with the interpretation and appropriation of the historical sections of Scripture. The problem may be posed in several ways. *How* is the book of Acts the word of God? That is, does it have a word which not only describes the primitive church but speaks as a norm to the church at all times? If there is such a word, how does one discover it, or set up principles in order to hear it? If the primitive church is normative, *which* expression of it is normative? Jerusalem? Antioch? Philippi? Corinth? That is, why do not all the churches sell their possessions and have all things in common? Or further, is it at all legitimate to take descriptive statements as normative? If so, how does one distinguish those which are from those which are not? For example, must we follow the pattern of Acts 1:26 and select leaders by lot? Just exactly what role does historical precedent play in Christian doctrine or in the understanding of Christian experience?

Already I have raised more questions than I am capable of answering. Unfortunately, one looks in vain in the standard works on hermeneutics for answers, because for the most part these questions are not asked.[15] Under the rubric of "special hermeneutics" one finds suggestions or principles on how to deal with prophecy, typology, parables, apocalypses, etc., but nothing on the manner in which one is to understand the historical sections as a normative word for today.[16] This is all

ment concerning the frequency of the Lord's Supper. Most Assemblies churches, therefore, observe the Supper monthly, although daily or weekly seems to be the biblical "pattern."

[15] [Since this essay was first published I have discovered a whole spate of literature on this subject in the Restoration movement (Disciples and Churches of Christ). Much of this has been supplied to me by Craig Beard, former reference librarian at Harding University, Searcy, Arkansas, and now at the University of Alabama at Birmingham. In contrast to the early Pentecostals, this movement has clearly seen that everything for them is hermeneutical and stands or falls on their ability to establish normative practice from the narratives of Scripture.]

[16] Paul D. Wieland offered a thesis to the Graduate School of Wheaton College entitled "Criteria for Determining the Normative in

the more surprising when one considers how often the Old Testament and New Testament historical and biographical sections are preached from not simply for illustrative value, but also somehow by analogy for normative value.

Since this is an exploratory essay, what follows is a potpourri of general hermeneutical observations and specific suggestions for the hermeneutics of historical precedent. These are not offered as definitive, but as an invitation to further dialogue both with my own Pentecostal brothers and sisters as well as with other evangelicals.[17]

III. General Principles of Biblical Hermeneutics

1. Issues of Genre

It should be an axiom of biblical hermeneutics that the interpreter must take into account the literary genre of the passage being interpreted, along with the questions of text, grammar, philology, and history. Such a principle would appear to be self-evident, yet it is seldom applied to the New Testament except for the Apocalypse. However, the Gospels, Epistles, and Acts are also distinct literary types, and awareness of this fact must become a part of valid hermeneutics.

The point is that not every biblical statement is the word of God in exactly the same way. That the Psalms are poetry, that the prophets are primarily a collection of spoken oracles, that Ecclesiastes and Job are Jewish wisdom literature,

New Testament Church Government" (1965). But he scarcely comes to grips with the issues raised here. He does have a long section on hermeneutics, which simply goes over much-plowed ground. In his (all too short) section on the hermeneutics of history he fails to distinguish between history as the mighty acts of God and as the mere recording of narrative events per se. He suggests that events in NT history may be exemplary, serving as models or warnings (p. 15), but he offers no discussion of the criteria to be used in determining in what way, if any, they are normative for us.

[17] Much of what follows may seem irrelevant to some of my Roman Catholic brothers and sisters, since historical precedent (as tradition) has for them a fixed role in establishing what is normative for the Christian faith.

that Daniel and the Revelation are apocalyptic, that the Epistles are letters, and that the Acts is historical narrative must be a primary consideration in interpretation in order to avoid the non-contextual, "promise box" approach to Scripture.

For example, the Epistles must be taken seriously as letters, not treated primarily as theological treatises. Theology obviously abounds—and frequently is the primary intent; but the Epistles are not systematic treatises on theology. Paul's theology is related to his special task as missionary to the Gentiles, and it is worked out accordingly.[18] This does not diminish the theological value of the Epistles—indeed, I think it enhances it—but it does demand that the interpreter be aware of the genre and not treat the writings of Paul in the same manner he or she would read the treatises of Augustine or the *Summa* of Aquinas.

So also with the Acts. However much of the "theology" of Luke one finds in the book, it is *not* an epistle or a theological treatise. Even if one disregards its historical value, one cannot, indeed must not, disregard the fact that it is cast in the form of historical narrative. This, it seems to me, is the great fault of the monumental works of Dibelius and Haenchen.[19] They tend to treat Acts first as theology and only secondarily as history. I demur. Theology there is aplenty, and theology is almost certainly part of Luke's intent; but it is cast as history, and the first principle of hermeneutics here is to take that literary genre seriously.

The significance of this principle for our problem is that in the hermeneutics of biblical history the major task of the interpreter is to discover the author's (I would add, the Holy Spirit's) *intent* in the recording of that history. This, of course, is a general maxim of hermeneutics and applies to the other literary genres as well. But it is of crucial importance to the hermeneutics of the historical narratives, for it is one thing for the historian to include an event because it serves the greater purpose of his work, and yet another thing for the

---

[18] Cf. G. W. Barker, W. L. Lane, J. R. Michaels, *The New Testament Speaks* (New York: Harper, 1969) 148–49.

[19] Martin Dibelius, *Studies in the Acts of the Apostles* (London: SCM, 1956); Ernst Haenchen, *The Acts of the Apostles* (Philadelphia: Westminster, 1971).

interpreter to take that incident as having didactic value apart from the historian's larger intent.

Although Luke's "broader intent" may be a moot point for some, it is a defensible hypothesis that he was trying to show how the church emerged as a chiefly Gentile, worldwide phenomenon from its origins as a Jerusalem-based, Judaism-oriented sect of Jewish believers, and how the Holy Spirit was ultimately responsible for this phenomenon of universal salvation based on grace alone.

An event such as the conversion of Cornelius serves this broader interest not simply to "represent a principle . . . of higher historical truth" (so Dibelius), nor simply to illustrate Christian conversion in general or the baptism in the Holy Spirit in particular (so Pentecostals). Rather, Cornelius serves for Luke as the first-fruits of the Gentile mission, and he is important to Luke's purpose because his conversion is by direct intervention of the Holy Spirit through one of the Jerusalem apostles (Acts 15:7; cf. 10:19, 44; 11:12; 15). Through these combined circumstances the eyes of the church were opened to the fact that "even to the Gentiles God has granted repentance unto life."

Whatever else one gleans from the story, whether it be the place of visions in Christian guidance (!) or the nature of Christian conversion, such gleanings are *incidental* to Luke's intent. This does not mean that what is incidental is false, that it has no theological value; it does mean that God's word for us in that narrative is primarily related to what it was intended to teach.[20]

On the basis of this discussion the following principles emerge with regard to hermeneutics of historical narrative:

(1) The word of God in Acts which may be regarded as normative for Christians is related primarily to what any given narrative was *intended* to teach.

---

[20] [Here is another place where Menzies, " Trends," expresses concern, suggesting that this view is "reductionist." Perhaps so, but my problem still remains—and Menzies' article only exacerbates it for me—and that is, how does one unpack or discover Luke's *theological* interests in his individual narratives, and how does one distinguish those he *intends* to be normative from those he does not, without his giving us some clue *in the text itself.* For further discussion see the Postscript below.]

(2) What is *incidental* to the primary intent of the narrative may indeed reflect an author's theology, or how he understood things, but it cannot have the same didactic value as what the narrative was *intended* to teach has. This does not negate what is incidental or imply that it has no word for us. What it does argue is that what is incidental must not become primary, although it may always serve as additional support to what is unequivocally taught elsewhere.

(3) Historical precedent, to have normative value, must be related to *intent*. That is, if it can be shown that the purpose of a given narrative is to *establish* precedent, then such precedent should be regarded as normative. For example, if it could be demonstrated on exegetical grounds that Luke's intent in Acts 1:15–26 was to give the church a precedent for selecting its leaders, then such a selection process should be followed by later Christians. But if the establishing of precedent was *not* the intent of the narrative, then its value as a precedent for later Christians should be treated according to the specific principles suggested in the next section of this essay.

2. Establishing Doctrine from Scripture

Closely related to the foregoing discussion is the observation that not all doctrinal statements derived from Scripture belong to the same categories, nor are they on the same level within those categories.

In general, doctrinal statements fall into three categories: (1) Christian theology (what Christians believe), (2) Christian ethics (how Christians ought to behave), and (3) Christian experience or practice (what Christians do in terms of religious practices). Statements within these categories may further be classified as primary or secondary, depending on whether, on the one hand, they are derived from what are "propositions" or "imperatives" (i.e., what is *intended*) or whether, on the other hand, they are derived incidentally, by implication or by precedent.[21]

---

[21] This, of course, does not rule out the didactic nature of the historical portions of Scripture. What we learn of God from his acts is every bit as important as what we learn from "propositions." These acts, which teach us of his reality and grace, are usually *interpreted* as

For example, in the category of Christian theology such statements as God is one, God is love, all have sinned, Christ died for sins, salvation is by grace, and Jesus Christ is divine are derived from passages where they are taught by intent, and are therefore primary. At the secondary level are those statements which are the logical outflow of the primary statements or are derived by implication from Scripture. Thus the fact, or "that-ness," of the deity of Christ is primary; *how* the natures concur in unity is secondary. A similar distinction may be made with regard to the doctrine of Scripture: that it is the inspired word of God is primary; the nature of the inspiration is secondary. This is not to say that the secondary statements are unimportant. Quite often they will have significant bearing on one's faith with regard to the primary statements. Their ultimate theological value may be related to how well they preserve the integrity of the primary statements.

Similar distinctions may be made in the category of Christian ethics. At the primary level are the general maxims, the imperatives, the absolutes: love for one's enemy, unlimited forgiveness, temperance, etc. From these may be derived concrete principles and applications for specific situations.

The concept of levels of doctrinal statements seems to apply as well to the category which is of special interest in this chapter: Christian experience and practice. For example, the necessity of the Lord's Supper is at the primary level, based on an imperative; but the frequency of its observance, which is based on precedent alone, is surely not as binding. So also with the necessity of baptism and its mode, or with the practice of Christians "assembling of themselves together" and the frequency or the day of the week. Again, this is not to say that the secondary statements are unimportant. For example, one will surely be hard pressed to prove that Christians must meet to worship on Saturday or Sunday; but in either case one is saying something of theological significance by one's practice.

The doctrine of a baptism in the Holy Spirit as subsequent to conversion and accompanied by tongues seems to

having didactic or saving significance. Thus we have Gospels, not simply collections of the sayings of Jesus. The saving events of history are a deed-word complex—not simply deed, nor simply word. Cf. George E. Ladd, *New Testament and Criticism*, 19–33.

belong to the secondary level of doctrinal statements in my third category. That believers are to be (or keep) filled with the Spirit, that they are to walk and live in the Spirit is at the primary level and normative. When and how one enters the dimension of Christian experience, although not unimportant, is not of the same "normative" quality, because the "when and how" is based solely on precedent and/or analogy.

IV. Specific Principles for the Use of Historical Precedent[22]

With these general observations and principles in view, I would offer the following suggestions as to the hermeneutics of historical precedent:

1. The Use of Analogy as Precedent

The use of historical precedent as an analogy by which to establish a norm is never valid in itself. Such a process (drawing universal norms from particular events) produces a *non sequitur* and is therefore irrelevant. Thus, to urge the necessity of water baptism as an act of obedience to Jesus' example is bad exegesis. John's baptism and Christian baptism, though the latter is probably rooted in the former, are different things, and the meaning and necessity of Christian baptism must be made of sterner stuff.

Likewise the analogies of Jesus and the apostles as having been "born" of the Spirit and later "baptized" in the Spirit may be interesting analogies, but they are of such a different kind from succeeding Christian experience that they can scarcely have normative value. The day of Pentecost is a great line of demarcation; it marks the beginning of the age of

---

[22] [R. Stronstad ("The Hermeneutics of Lucan Historiography," *Paraclete* 22 [Fall 1988] 10) has suggested that this articulation of principles "hedges" what I have written to this point, which is "little more than a sophisticated echo of Stott." He also suggests (p. 9) that this articulation "radically limits the normative and precedent value of historical narrative." Perhaps the issue has to do with my understanding of the words "precedent" and "normative." In any case, for further discussion of this issue see the Postscript below (section VI).]

the Spirit. Surely valid patterns of *Christian* experience must follow that day, not precede it.

2. Historical Narrative as Illustration and Pattern

Although it may not have been the author's primary purpose, historical narratives do have illustrative and, sometimes, "pattern" value. In fact, this is how the New Testament people used the historical narratives of the Old Testament. Paul, for example, used certain Old Testament examples as warnings to those who had a false security in their divine election (1 Cor 10:1–13); and Jesus used the example of David as a historical precedent to justify his disciples' sabbath actions (Mark 2:23–28 and parallels).

Whether we can reproduce the manner of exegesis which the New Testament authors applied to the Old Testament may be a moot point.[23] It should be noted, however, especially in cases where the precedent justifies a present action, that the precedent does not establish a norm for specific action. People are not to eat regularly of the show-bread or to pluck grain on the sabbath to show that the sabbath was made for man. Rather, the precedent illustrates a principle with regard to the sabbath.

A caveat is in order here: for a biblical precedent to justify a present action, the principle of the action must be taught elsewhere, where it is the primary intent so to teach. For example, to use Jesus' cleansing of the temple to justify one's so-called righteous indignation—usually a euphemism for selfish anger—is to abuse this principle. On the other hand, the Pentecostal may justify his or her speaking in tongues not only from precedent (in Acts) but also from the teaching about spiritual gifts in 1 Corinthians 12–14.

3. Historical Narratives as Repeatable Patterns

In matters of Christian experience, and even more so of Christian practice, biblical precedents may be regarded as

---

[23] Richard N. Longenecker ("Can We Reproduce the Exegesis of the New Testament?" *Tyndale Bulletin* 21 [1970] 3–38) has argued that because of the revelatory character of the NT its exegesis should be considered "once-for-all," not normative, and in some cases not even repeatable.

repeatable patterns—even if they are not to be regarded as normative. This is especially true when the practice itself is mandatory but the mode is not.

The repeatable character of certain practices or patterns should be guided by the following considerations:

a. The strongest possible case can be made when only one pattern is found (although one must be careful not to make too much of silence), and when the pattern is repeated within the New Testament itself.

b. When there is an ambiguity of patterns or when a pattern occurs but once, it is repeatable for later Christians only if it appears to have divine approbation or is in harmony with what is taught elsewhere in Scripture.

c. What is culturally conditioned is either not repeatable at all, or must be translated into the new or differing culture.

Thus, on the basis of these principles, one can make the strongest kind of case for immersion as the mode of baptism, a much weaker case for the observance of the Lord's Supper each Sunday, and almost no case, except on other grounds, for infant baptism.[24] By the same token, the Mormon practice of baptism for the dead fails on all counts.

It is in the light of such principles, and in keeping with the careful exegesis of all passages involved, that one must examine the Pentecostal "distinctives."

V. Pentecostal Distinctives and Historical Precedent[25]

The question of a baptism in the Holy Spirit distinct from and subsequent to conversion remains a thorny one. In the first place, the Pentecostal has indeed experienced such a "baptism," and for him or her it has had a dynamic quality similar to the life in the Spirit one finds in the Acts. But apart from the analogies of Jesus and the apostles (ruled out as ultimately irrelevant), the Pentecostal's biblical support for

---

[24] Infant baptism, of course, may be argued from historical precedent, but not so easily from the *biblical* historical precedent, which is the issue here.
[25] [See now the considerable elaboration of this material in chapter 7.]

this baptism as "subsequent to and distinct from" rests on the "pattern" of Samaria (two weeks?), Paul (three days), and Ephesus (several minutes?). When faced with the Cornelius episode, the Pentecostal has argued either that Cornelius was already a Christian as a god-fearer (surely a case of special pleading) or that "this visitation was God's ideal, his perfect pattern: believe Christ, receive the Holy Spirit in immediate succession."[26]

The Pentecostal's strongest case is the episode at Samaria (Acts 8), but whether Luke intended to imply an experience "distinct from" conversion is debatable. Some indeed have argued against the Pentecostals (weakly, it seems to me) that the Samaritans were not even Christians until the advent of the Spirit (18:17).[27] However, there are too many terms denoting Christian experience prior to verse 17 to give this view much support. Such terms as "[they] with one accord gave heed to what was said" (v. 6), had "much joy" (v. 8), "believed Philip as he preached the good news" (v. 12), "were baptized" (v. 12), and "had received the word of God" (v. 14) are used elsewhere by Luke to describe the Christian experience of conversion. To argue on the basis of Romans 8:1–17 that they do not do so here seems also to be a case of special pleading. Luke surely intended to be describing believers.

Yet the Holy Spirit "had not yet fallen on them" (v. 16). Is Luke thereby *intending to teach* "distinct from and subsequent to"? Probably not. It is furthermore questionable whether he is teaching it incidentally—at least the notion that a baptism in the Spirit is distinct from conversion. In a carefully argued exegetical study of all relevant passages in Acts, Dunn concluded that for Luke the real evidence (and chief element) of Christian experience was the presence of the Spirit. What seems to be important for Luke in this narrative is that the validation (and completion) of the Christian experience in the initial spread beyond Jerusalem is tied to the Jerusalem church and signified by a dynamic quality similar to theirs. If this is a correct understanding of Luke's concern, and it surely is defensible exegesis, then the concept of subsequence is

[26] Riggs, *The Spirit Himself,* 111.
[27] See Dunn, *Baptism,* 55–72.

irrelevant. What is of consequence is the experiential, dynamic quality of the gift of the Spirit.

If, however, a baptism in the Spirit "distinct from and subsequent to" is neither clearly taught in the New Testament nor necessarily to be seen as a normative pattern (let alone the *only* pattern) for Christian experience, there is a pattern in Acts which *may* be derived only from historical precedent by the intent of Luke and Paul.

It would seem from any valid reading of Luke and Paul that the gift of the Spirit was not some sort of adjunct to Christian experience, nor was it some kind of second and more significant part of Christian experience. It was rather the chief element of Christian life, from beginning to end. Everywhere for Luke it is the presence of the Spirit that signifies the "real thing." And Paul asks the Galatians as to their Christian experience, "Did you receive the Spirit by works of the law, or by hearing with faith?" (Gal 3:2). Furthermore, in Acts the recurring pattern of the coming (or presence) of the Spirit has a dramatic, or dynamic, element to it. It was experienced, or to use contemporary parlance, it was very often *charismatic* in nature.

If in the attempt to recapture this New Testament pattern, the Pentecostal saw the dynamic element as "distinct from and subsequent to," he or she should not thereby be faulted. The fault perhaps lay with the church which no longer normally expected or experienced life in the Spirit in a dynamic way.

The question as to whether tongues is the initial physical evidence of the charismatic quality of life in the Spirit is a moot point. Some Pentecostals see speaking in tongues as a repeated pattern and have argued that it is *the* normal pattern. Others agree that it is a repeated, and therefore repeatable pattern; but to insist that it is the only valid sign seems to place too much weight on the historical precedent of three (perhaps four) instances in Acts.

What, then, may the Pentecostal say about his or her experience in view of the hermeneutical principles suggested in this paper?

(1) In the New Testament the presence of the Spirit was the chief element of Christian conversion and the Christian life.

(2) In Acts, as well as in the Pauline churches (cf. 1 Thess 5:19–21; 1 Cor 12–14), a charismatic dimension was a normal phenomenon in the reception of the Spirit.

(3) Speaking in tongues, if not normative, was a repeated expression of the charismatic dimension of the coming of the Spirit. Given Paul's clearly congenial attitude toward this phenomenon in 1 Corinthians 12–14,[28] both with regard to himself and to the Corinthians, Pentecostals have much in their favor to argue that this was the *normal* (in the sense of *expected*) experience of believers in the early church.[29]

(4) Even though most contemporary Christians no longer expect a charismatic dimension *as an integral part of their conversion*, they may nevertheless—on the basis of the New Testament pattern—still experience such a dimension of life in the Spirit. That this dimension is now usually subsequent to conversion is ultimately irrelevant. The charismatic dimension is a repeatable, and—the Pentecostal would argue—a valuable dimension of life in the Spirit.

(5) Since speaking in tongues was a repeated expression of this dynamic, or charismatic, dimension of the coming of the Spirit, the contemporary Christian may expect this, too, as a part of his or her experience in the Spirit. If the Pentecostal may not say one *must* speak in tongues, the Pentecostal may surely say, why *not* speak in tongues? It does have repeated biblical precedent, it did have evidential value at Cornelius' household (Acts 10:45–46), and—in spite of much that has been written to the contrary—it does have value both for the edification of the believer (1 Cor 14:2–4) and, with interpretation, for the edification of the church (1 Cor 14:5, 26–28).

---

[28] Contrary to some, Paul is not "condemning tongues with faint praise." That is to belittle what he says very matter-of-factly in 14:19 about his own personal spirituality. The issue in Corinth is one of correcting an abuse, not eliminating a nuisance.

[29] [This last sentence has been added in the present edition, as a way of saying more strongly what I believe to be the strength of the Pentecostal position.]

VI. A Postscript

Since this essay invited dialogue with other Pentecostals, this republication gives me an opportunity briefly to join in such dialogue with two colleagues, and good friends, William Menzies[30] and Roger Stronstad,[31] who have taken my invitation seriously. Rather than here replay their critiques and respond to them point by point, I invite the reader to read Menzies and Stronstad for herself/himself. What I wish to do here is to respond to what I perceive as the basic issues they have raised: (1) whether theology may be derived from biblical narrative, even if not clearly taught elsewhere by intent; (2) the semantics of "normal," "normative," and "precedent," by which I assumed certain understandings that may not have been true of my colleagues; and (3) the matter of Luke's intentionality with regard to the basic "Pentecostal narratives" in question. The following response is not intended to defend my own positions; rather I hope to clarify—or modify as necessary—my stated positions and thus to advance the dialogue.

1. Deriving Theology from Narrative

Both Menzies and Stronstad express concern that my "general principles" in Part III are too "reductionist" (Menzies) or "radically limiting" (Stronstad). In the case of Stronstad this is related even more to some explicit statements in chapter 6 of *How to Read the Bible for All Its Worth* that seem to suggest that "historical narrative can only have didactic value when its message is taught elsewhere, specifically in the teaching of Jesus, or in the sermons or writings of the apostles."[32]

---

[30] See "Synoptic Theology, An Essay on Pentecostal Hermeneutics," *Paraclete* 13 (Winter 1979) 14–21; a revised edition of this paper appeared as "The Methodology of Pentecostal Theology: An Essay on Hermeneutics," in *Essays on Apostolic Themes: Studies in Honor of Howard M. Ervin* (ed. P. Elbert; Peabody Mass.: Hendrickson, 1985) 1–14.

[31] In Parts One and Two of a series of lectures given at the Assemblies of God Theological Seminary, Springfield Mo., and subsequently published in *Paraclete*: "Trends in Pentecostal Hermeneutics," 22 (Summer 1988) 1–12; "The Hermeneutics of Lucan Historiography," 22 (Fall 1988) 5–17.

I do not deny that some real differences may exist between us here; but we do not all mean the same thing by "didactic." I strongly agree with both colleagues, and especially with Stronstad, on the "charismatic nature" of Lukan theology; moreover, I am equally convinced, with Stronstad, that this theology, derived largely from narratives, is equally "normative"—and thus "didactic"—in its significance for later Christian theology as are the Epistles of Paul.[33] But such theology, again as Stronstad argues vigorously, is the result of careful study of the whole of Luke–Acts, not simply from a few or several individual narratives—although the latter obviously play their part in the larger whole.

My concern lies in two areas, and here I probably do differ with Menzies in particular. First, it is not "theology" in the larger sense that concerns me, but the concept of "didactic" as it is related specifically to the question of establishing specific *patterns* of Christian experience and practice as *norms*. It is the issue of "specific patterns of Christian experience and practice" that called forth the second part of the argument in Section III. I do not deny that we are saying something theological by our praxis, but I doubt whether this is an area of theology of the same kind as what I have called "theology proper" and "ethics."

Second, I have a concern over the question of "norms" or "normative," especially in the area of Christian experience and practice. But this leads to the second major issue that my colleagues have raised with me.

2. The Semantics of "Normal," "Normative," and "Precedent"

My experience in the larger church, both evangelical and Pentecostal, is what led directly to the writing of this essay. I was teaching at Wheaton College at the time, and regularly heard chapel speakers appeal to various narratives or examples from both the Old and New Testaments as "establishing precedent for us." I often wondered what that meant.

---

[32] "Hermeneutics," 10.

[33] In some ways this is exactly the point I try to make in the next essay in a slightly different way for the whole NT.

My guess is that most often it meant something close to "repeatable," that is, that the biblical people did something that we would do well to pattern our lives after. On the other hand, it was also clear that at times they meant something much closer to what I would call "normative."

Menzies has especially expressed concern that by my own distinctions between "normal," "normative," and "repeatable" I would water down the Pentecostal position too much. "Repeatable is hardly a preachable item," he suggests[34]—although my experience at Wheaton and elsewhere suggests otherwise. In any case, the concern is that if a pattern is "merely repeatable" most people will scarcely give it a second thought, and for many believers that means continuing on in the present "norm" of anemia.[35] Since as a Pentecostal I share this concern, let me try at least to clarify my use of these words, as an attempt both to explain where I am coming from and to bring greater precision to the discussion.

The language "establishing a norm," and therefore for something to be "normative," I have always understood to refer to what must be adhered to by all Christians at all times and in all places, if they are truly to be obedient to God's word. It becomes a matter of obedience, pure and simple.

By "normal" I mean what I take Article 7 in the Assemblies of God creed to mean when it says that "this was the normal experience of all in the early Christian Church." I understand that to suggest that this is the way it was for them, as a normal, expected, recurring experience. My colleagues in New Testament scholarship may disagree with me here, but I am convinced that the dynamic, empowering dimension of life in the Spirit was the "norm" in the early church, and that they simply would not have understood the less-than-dynamic quality of life in the Spirit (without the Spirit?) that has been the "norm" of so much of the later church. Precisely because it was "normal" in this sense, it was the *presupposition* of life in the Spirit for them; thus they felt no compulsion to talk about it at every turn.

---

[34] "Methodology," 10.
[35] These are my words, not Menzies', although I think this gets at the heart of the issue.

Precisely because I understand this dimension of life in the Spirit to be the New Testament norm, I think it is repeatable, and should be so, as the norm of the later church. Where I would tend to disagree with my tradition in the articulation of this norm is when they use language that seems more obligatory to me than I find in the New Testament documents themselves.[36]

3. Lukan Intentionality

Finally there is the methodological issue that all three of us dance around a bit, that of finding Luke's own intent in his various narratives. As Stronstad puts it, rather strongly, "Concerning Luke's narratives about the Holy Spirit, who determines authorial intent—Pentecostals or non-Pentecostals? . . . Who is authorized to adjudicate between Pentecostals and their opponents whether or not Luke may teach 20th century Christians about their experience of the Holy Spirit?"[37]

This is an issue on which I would love to work within some kind of community setting, since here in particular I surely have neither the first nor last word. What I would like to offer to the discussion is a twofold agenda: (1) It seems to me that we must first speak to the question of whether or not one is justified at all in assuming that there *is* a doctrinal/theological *imperative* in Luke's narratives, with regard to repeating the specifics. Especially so, since Luke does not seem to specify anywhere that he intends his history to be precedent for the church in some way. (2) Since there seems to be a considerable diversity of patterns within Acts itself, how therefore does one distinguish among them as to the "normative" ones? If in fact normativeness were Luke's concern in the matter of individual narratives, how does one explain his failure to narrate every instance of the same kind of experience in the same way?

I would not want to say that Luke did *not* intend us to understand the baptism of the Spirit to be distinct from and

---

[36] I should mention here that in private conversation and correspondence with Bill Menzies some of our apparent disagreements on this matter seem to have been cleared up.
[37] "Hermeneutics," 11.

subsequent to conversion, intended for empowering, and always evidenced by speaking in tongues; I simply am less convinced than my Pentecostal forebears that Luke did so intend. And chiefly because, even though this pattern can be found in three (probably four, and perhaps five) instances, it is clearly not expressly narrated in this way in every instance. Although I am quite open on this question, I do not find in Menzies' articles the kinds of criteria that help me to think otherwise on this matter.

But in any case, my long experience in evangelical settings makes me urge that we articulate our hermeneutics in such a way that these friends will find it at least viable, if not always compelling. If we cannot do so, it may in fact be a question of their own biases at work. On the other hand, we need always to ask whether or not it is ours instead. I for one am convinced that our experience approximates that of the early church, and that others would do well so to experience the Spirit of the living God. And therefore I am willing to continue to wrestle with the articulation of our hermeneutics, so that we do justice both to Scripture and to the ongoing experience of the Spirit in the church.

7

BAPTISM IN THE HOLY SPIRIT: THE ISSUE OF SEPARABILITY AND SUBSEQUENCE

Article 7 of the "Statement of Fundamental Truths" in the constitution and by-laws of the General Council of the Assemblies of God reads:

> All believers are entitled to and should ardently expect and earnestly seek the promise of the Father, the baptism in the Holy Ghost and fire, according to the command of our Lord Jesus Christ. This was the normal experience of all in the early Christian Church. With it comes the enduement of power for life and service, the bestowment of the gifts and their uses in the work of the ministry (Luke 24:49; Acts 1:4, 8; I Corinthians 12:1–3). This experience is distinct from and subsequent to the experience of the new birth (Acts 8:12–17; 10:44–46; 11:14–16; 15:7–9).

The theological sentiment expressed in this statement, it should be noted, is not unique to Pentecostalism. Rather, it reflects a classical view of many pietistic groups, reaching at least as far back as early Methodism, and found subsequently in various holiness and deeper life movements, namely, that there is for all believers a "baptism in the Holy Spirit," which is separate from and sequential to the initial experience of conversion. Indeed two of the best known defenses of this position were written by none other than the first president of Moody

Bible Institute, R. A. Torrey, and one of the founders of Gordon-Conwell Theological Seminary, A. J. Gordon.[1] The uniquely Pentecostal contribution to this theological construct was to insist on the gift of tongues as the evidential sign that such a baptism had indeed taken place, and to insist on the empowering-for-service dimension of the experience.[2]

Since Pentecostals experienced this "baptism" after their conversion, they have also regularly argued for the *biblical* nature of *both* their experience of baptism *and* its timing (as separate and subsequent). And since they tend to make the *timing* of the experience of equal significance to the experience itself,[3] those who have opposed the Pentecostal position have also generally believed themselves to have dealt a crippling blow to the Pentecostalism when they have argued exegetically against its timing (as the Pentecostals express it).[4]

The purpose of this present essay is to open the question of separability and subsequence once again, and (1) to suggest that there is in fact very little *biblical* support for the traditional Pentecostal position on this matter, but (2) to argue further that this is of little real consequence to the doc-

---

[1] See R. A. Torrey, *The Baptism with the Holy Spirit* (New York: Revell, 1897), and A. J. Gordon, *The Ministry of the Spirit* (Philadelphia: American Baptist Publication Society, 1894).

[2] For the matter of tongues, see especially Article 8 in the Assemblies of God "Statement of Fundamental Truths," cited above in chapter 6 (p. 84). See Article 7 quoted above for a statement about empowering for service. [R. Stronstad, "Trends," 7, has suggested that in this essay, "in violation of [my] own caution about elevating incidental things to a primary position, [I] have done this on the subjects of separability and subsequence." This, of course, is not my intent. The primary issue for classical Pentecostalism has always been the "empowering-for-service" dimension of the baptism in the Spirit. But it is also clear in the literature that distinction, and therefore subsequence (see e.g., Menzies' critique in the Ervin *Festschrift* ["Methodology," 11), is a continuing concern in Pentecostal theology. In any case, my point is a simple one; it is not to discover and to speak to the primary issue, but simply to discuss an issue that lies close to the center of classical Pentecostalism's articulation of its experience of the Spirit.]

[3] [This is overstated, and leaves me open to the charge leveled by Stronstad (preceding note). My point here is simply that it is crucial to Pentecostal theology that the enduement of power does *not* take place at conversion. Pentecostals were led to this emphasis both by their own experience and later in response to criticism from the outside.]

[4] See, e.g., Bruner, *Theology*, 153–218.

trine of the baptism in the Holy Spirit, either as to the validity of the experience itself or to its articulation.

I. The Pentecostal and the Baptism in the Spirit

In order to understand the doctrine of "subsequence" one must first try to understand the Pentecostals themselves—and how this doctrinal stance came to be so cherished.

Pentecostals have often been accused of exegeting their own experience and then looking to the Bible to support it.[5] In part this may be true; but it is important to know *why* they have done so. On the one hand, their experience itself has been so empowering, so thoroughly life-changing, both in terms of personal obedience to God and readiness and empowerment for witness, that they instinctively know that it *must* be of God—and therefore must be biblical.

But since, on the other hand, for *them* that experience was subsequent to their conversion, they turned to the New Testament for the basis *both* of the experience itself *and* its timing. Their reasons for this are clear. All the early Pentecostals carried with them to their experience the traditional Protestant view of Scripture, as inspired *of* the Spirit and made effective *by* the Spirit through Spirit-anointed preaching. Thus the Pentecostals felt a great urgency to verify their experience by the interpretation of Scripture. For them the Bible was still central; and since their own experience of the Spirit was so vital, they knew that the God of the Bible and the God of their experience had to be the *one God*. Hence they automatically expected to find the evidence for their experience in Scripture. Their understanding of Scripture, therefore, seemed both reasonable—and perfectly plain.

In the course of articulating this experience biblically, however, they felt a special urgency to press for *all* the aspects of the experience—not only the experience itself, but also especially its necessity as a work of grace subsequent to sal-

---

[5] [I have suggested as much myself; see the preceding chapter, p. 86. But as noted there, it is only "in a sense" that they do so. As pointed out in chapter 5, their experience came originally as a direct result of searching the Scriptures.]

vation. But in so doing, they exposed their flanks to some exegetical and hermeneutical weaknesses; and they ended up trying to persuade others of the rightness of their experience on grounds different from their *own* experience of the Spirit.

The Pentecostal experience historically came out of a deep dissatisfaction with "things as they are" in light of "things as they were" in the New Testament church, plus a deep spiritual hunger for the latter. They belonged to that tradition of piety that cried out, "O God, fill me with yourself and your power or I die." Out of that hunger and cry, they experienced a mighty encounter with God the Holy Spirit. Then they turned around (especially in the second generation) and tried to bring others, many of whom did not share the same dissatisfaction or deep spiritual hunger, to their same experience through the more cerebral route of a biblical apologetic; they thus became, in a sense, a kind of living contradiction.

What I hope to show in the rest of this essay is that the Pentecostals are generally right on target biblically as to their *experience* of the Spirit. Their difficulties arose from the attempt to defend it biblically at the wrong point.

It should be noted here that the biblical support for the concepts of separability and subsequence is basically two-fold: (1) The use of biblical analogies (Jesus himself, who was born of the Spirit and was subsequently anointed of the Spirit at his baptism, and the apostles, who had Jesus breathe on them on Easter Day [interpreted as regeneration] and were subsequently baptized in the Spirit at Pentecost); and (2) the use of biblical precedent in the book of Acts (in Samaria [Acts 8], in Paul [Acts 9], and in Ephesus [Acts 19]).

Although a number of things can be said in the Pentecostal's favor for some of this, there are several clear exegetical/hermeneutical weaknesses in the classical presentation:

1. Arguments from Biblical Analogies

Arguments from biblical analogies are especially tenuous. They may function well in preaching, but for theology they serve less well, for at least two reasons:

a. The whole question of intentionality becomes a crucial one here. It can seldom be demonstrated that our analogies are intentional in the biblical text itself, as it was inspired by the Holy Spirit. Indeed it is more likely that they are irrelevant altogether.

b. Furthermore, it will be difficult to gain universal agreement on what, in fact, in the biblical text does serve as an appropriate analogy. It seems to me that no one can easily deny the importance of the descent of the Spirit on Jesus at his baptism. But it will be equally difficult to get very many people to see the appropriateness of the relationship of that event to his birth as analogy for subsequent Christian experience. Likewise, the uniqueness of the event of Pentecost in salvation history, not to mention the exegetical difficulties of demonstrating that John 20:22 refers to a regenerational experience, makes that analogy equally tenuous—although, again, who will deny the significance of the event of Pentecost for the apostolic ministry.

Analogies, therefore, are just that—analogies. But they can scarcely be treated as the biblical stuff on which to build Christian theology.

2. The Function of Biblical Precedent

On the second matter, the function of biblical precedent for the construction of Christian theology, I have already had much to say.[6] Let me here repeat my own conclusions. Events narrated in Scripture that have clear divine approbation, and especially when there is a repeated pattern, have the highest level of viability as repeatable patterns in the ongoing church. The problem occurs when one would elevate such patterns to be mandatory patterns—necessarily repeated or otherwise one is sub-biblical in some way.

Moreover, in the case of the three narratives of Acts, there are some exegetical concerns as well, as to whether they *intend* what Pentecostals see in them. For example, it is extremely unlikely, despite his use of *mathētai* to describe them, that Luke intended us to see the people in Acts 19 as Christians in any real sense, especially since they knew nothing of the coming of the Spirit, the *sine qua non* of truly Christian experience, and since they received Christian baptism at

[6] See the preceding chapter; cf. Fee and Stuart, *How to Read*, 87–102.

this point, implying that their previous baptism was *not* Christian.

The narratives of the Samaritan's and Paul's conversions do indeed reflect the coming of the Spirit as subsequent to what appears to be the actual experience of conversion. But the problems here are several. In the Samaritan case, for example, Luke actually says the Spirit does not come on them until the laying on of the apostles' hands. In order to square this with Paul's statement in Romans 8, James Dunn has argued that Luke does not consider them to be genuine believers before that.[7] But that seems to run aground on the rest of linguistic evidence used to describe them prior to the laying on of hands, all of which is Lukan language for Christian conversion.[8] Indeed the resolution to this tension is most likely to be found at the linguistic level. One simply must not press Luke's phenomenological use of Spirit language into service for theological precision. Although Luke *says* otherwise, we may assume the Samaritans and Paul to have become believers in the Pauline sense—that without the Spirit they are none of his. For Luke, however, the phenomenological expressions of the Spirit's presence are what he describes as the "coming of" or "filling with" the Spirit.

Thus in the case of Samaria, the Pentecostals do seem to have a biblical precedent, both for subsequence and, almost certainly, for tongues as evidence. But is this single precedent the intended divine pattern, or is it, as most New Testament scholars think, a unique event in the early history? And in any case, why does it serve as a better precedent than Cornelius or Ephesus?

In thus arguing, as a New Testament scholar, against some cherished Pentecostal interpretations, I have in no sense abandoned what is essential to Pentecostalism. I have only tried to point out some inherent flaws in some of our historic

---

[7] Dunn, *Baptism*, 55–72.
[8] Dunn himself acknowledges this; his difficulty arises in starting with Paul and trying to fit Luke into that theological mold [cf. the similar critique in R. Stronstad, *The Charismatic Theology of St. Luke* (Peabody Mass.: Hendrickson, 1984) 9–12]. This forces him to say that the language must mean something slightly different here. On this matter see I. H. Marshall, *The Acts of the Apostles* (TNTC; Grand Rapids: Eerdmans, 1980) 154–56.

understanding of texts. The essential matter, after all, is neither subsequence nor tongues, but the Spirit himself as a dynamic, empowering presence; and there seems to me to be little question that our way of initiation into that—through an experience of Spirit baptism—has biblical validity. Whether all *must* go that route seems to me to be more moot; but in any case, the Pentecostal experience itself can be defended on exegetical grounds as a thoroughly biblical phenomenon. And to that I now turn.

II. The Holy Spirit in the New Testament

I think it is fair to note that if there is one thing that differentiates the early church from its twentieth-century counterpart it is in the level of awareness and experience of the presence and power of the Holy Spirit. Ask any number of people today from all sectors of Christendom to define or describe Christian conversion or Christian life, and the most noticeable feature of that definition would be its general lack of emphasis on the active, dynamic role of the Spirit.

It is precisely the opposite in the New Testament. The Spirit is no mere addendum. Indeed, he is the *sine qua non*, the essential ingredient, of Christian life. Nor is he a mere datum of theology; rather, he is *experienced* as a powerful presence in their lives. Whatever else may be said of the early church, it was first and foremost comprised of people of the Spirit.

In order for us to understand early Christians on this matter, we must appreciate the essentially eschatological nature of their existence and their understanding of the Spirit. For them, in a way that very few of us can fully appreciate, the Spirit was an eschatological reality—the clear evidence, the sure sign, that the coming age had dawned, that God had set the future inexorably in motion, to be consummated by a second coming of the Messiah. Thus for Paul the Spirit was the *arrabōn*, the down payment, on the future reality that was itself guaranteed by the down payment (2 Cor 1:21–22; 5:5; Eph 1:13–14). And for Luke the outpouring of the Spirit on the day of Pentecost was the eschatological fulfillment of the prophecy of Joel. So much is this so that in the Joel quotation in the Peter speech he alters the words "after these things" to "in the last days."[9]

Such an understanding, of course, is a reflection of contemporary expectations, which were based on a twofold understanding of messianic hopes: (1) that in the coming age the Messiah would be the unique *bearer* of the Spirit, as expressed in the prophecies of Isaiah 11:1–2; 42:1; and 61:1–3 (thus reflecting one of the Old Testament motifs of the Spirit, that he was necessary for leadership in Israel); and (2) that a part of the new covenant that would be ratified in the coming age would be the outpouring of the Spirit on all of God's people (e.g., Ezek 36:26–27; Joel 2:28–30, thus reflecting the other Old Testament motif that the Spirit was responsible for all genuine prophecy).

These eschatological expectations had been intensified during the intertestamental period by a theology of the "quenched Spirit," in which the present was seen as a time in which there was no Spirit in the land—hence the failure of the succession of the prophets[10]—and in which the Spirit was thus pushed into the future as the ultimate expression of the coming age.

It is precisely within this context that we are to understand the ministry of John the Baptist. According to Luke, he was filled with the Spirit from birth (1:15), and he grew and became strong in the Spirit (1:80), thus indicating a renewal of the prophetic tradition. In his own announcement of the coming Messiah the two great prophetic themes combine: "I saw the Spirit come down from heaven as a dove and remain on him. I would not have known him, except that the one who sent me to baptize with water told me 'The Man on whom you see *the Spirit come down and remain* is he who *will baptize with the Holy Spirit*' " (John 1:32–33). Thus in Luke 3:16, when asked whether he himself was the promised Messiah, John

---

[9] Haenchen, *Acts*, 179, argues that the text of B (*meta tauta*) is original on the grounds that "in Lukan theology the last days do not begin as soon as the Spirit has been outpoured." Here is a clear case of one's theology (Conzelmann's, in this case) prejudging one's historical sense. It is this text that refutes Haenchen and Conzelmann.

[10] See, e.g., Zech 13:2–3. During the intertestamental period this understanding is reflected in 1 Maccabees 9:37; 2 Baruch 85:3; and Josephus, *Against Apion* 1.41.

emphatically denied it in terms of the Spirit which the Messiah would pour out on all people: "I baptize with water. But one more powerful than I will come. . . . He will baptize you with the Holy Spirit and with fire." John thus coined the term, "baptism in the Holy Spirit," as a metaphor taken from his own sphere of activity; and he did so in order to contrast his own ministry with that of the Messiah who would usher in the coming age, the age of the Spirit. Although the prophetic hope, of course, had in it the promise of the Spirit for all people individually, that is not the emphasis in the metaphor itself. Rather, it is John's way of speaking of the Messiah's most essential quality, namely, that he would usher in the messianic age as the age of the Spirit.

Thus the Spirit in the New Testament is an eschatological reality. The Spirit belongs to the future, to the Age to Come. This is the key to everything in the New Testament. What is essential to understanding the ministry of Jesus is that he announced that with his own coming the kingdom of God, the coming age of righteousness and justice, had already begun. In the synagogue at Nazareth, the messianic prophecy of Isaiah 61:1, that the Spirit would rest upon the Messiah to bring justice and the time of God's favor, is announced to be fulfilled "in your hearing" (Luke 4:16–21). When accused of casting out demons by the power of Beelzebul, he announces, "If I by the Spirit of God cast out demons, then the kingdom (the Rule) of God has come present upon you" (Matt 12:28).

The Spirit is crucial to all of this. For Jesus himself, divine though he is, the key to his truly human life was the presence and fullness of the Spirit (Luke 4:14, 16; 5:17; Acts 2:22; 10:38). With him, the Messiah—the one uniquely anointed with the Spirit and power—had come. But it was only the dawning of the coming age, the beginning of the End, the inauguration of the Rule. Therefore, the power is there, but it is held in tension as veiled power—there for others, while he himself experienced weakness, servanthood, deprivation, and finally crucifixion. This is followed by resurrection. Surely now comes the End: "Will you now restore the kingdom to Israel?" That's the wrong question, Jesus implies. It is for you to receive power, when the Spirit comes, so that you may be witnesses to me.

It is in the context of all this that we are to understand the outpouring on the day of Pentecost. Above all else, the coming of the Spirit meant that God's people *also* had been ushered into the coming age. "This is that," shouts Peter. "The Spirit is here; the Age to Come has begun."

What we *must* understand is that the Spirit was the chief element, the primary ingredient, of this new existence. For early believers, it was not merely a matter of getting saved, forgiven, prepared for heaven. It was above all else to receive the Spirit, to walk into the coming age with *power*. They scarcely would have understood our Pentecostal terminology—"Spirit-filled Christian." That would be like saying "Scandinavian Swede." They simply did not think of Christian initiation as a two-stage process. For them, to be Christian meant to have the Spirit, to be a "Spirit person." To be "spiritual," therefore, did *not* mean to be some kind of special Christian, a Christian elitist (except perhaps at Corinth, where that was their failure). For them, to be spiritual meant to be a Christian—not over against a nominal (or carnal, etc.) Christian, but over against a non-Christian, one who does not have the Spirit.

The evidence for this is thoroughgoing in the New Testament. Everywhere in Luke–Acts it is the presence of the Spirit that marks off the people of the Age to Come. That is exactly the point of Paul's question in Acts 19:2. There were obviously not Christians because the one essential ingredient was missing. So also in John. It is the Spirit that will mark the people who believe and who are thus destined for eternal life (John 7:37–39; etc.).

And of course in Paul it is also everywhere. In 1 Corinthians 12:13, when trying to establish how it is that all of them have become one body in Christ, he singles out two metaphors for fullness of the Spirit—all have been immersed in the same reality, Spirit, and all have been made to drink to the fill of the same reality, Spirit. In Galatians, to counter the heresy of the Judaizers, at the start of the argument proper in chapter 3, he asks the one crucial question: "I would like to learn just one thing from you: Did you receive the Spirit by observing the law, or by believing what you heard?" This was clearly his way of asking about their experience of *becoming* Christians; and in vv. 4–5 he argues the same point from their present manifold experience of the Spirit, including the ongoing presence of miracles. So also in 1 Corinthians 2:6–16, where Paul sets out to contrast the Christian from non-Christian concerning why one can penetrate to the wisdom of the cross while the other cannot. The reason is that one has the Spirit; the other does not. That is, one is a Christian; the other is not. Likewise, in Romans 8, the whole point is that there are two kinds of existence: the one, *kata sarka*, means to live under the old order, under law; the other, *kata pneuma*, describes life as it is lived in the new age (cf. 2 Cor 5:14–17). Thus the basic imperative for Paul is not "Love one another" but is found in Galatians 5:16: "Walk in the Spirit."

Note, finally, that nowhere does the New Testament say, "Get saved, and then be filled with the Spirit." To early believers, getting saved, which included repentance and forgiveness obviously, meant especially to be filled with the Spirit. That all believers in Christ are Spirit-filled is the *presupposition* of the New Testament writers. Thus the imperative is, "Keep on being full of the Holy Spirit" (Eph 5:18).

On this analysis of things, it seems to me, all New Testament scholars would be in general agreement. But there is one further factor that must be noted, and perhaps here some will part company with me. Because for most Christians in the history of the church the Spirit was believed in but scarcely experienced as a powerful presence, either in the individual life or in the community, there grew up the idea that the Spirit was a quite unobtrusive presence. For the earliest Christians, it was quite the opposite. The Spirit was always thought of as a powerful presence. Indeed the terms Spirit and power at times are nearly interchangeable.[11] For the earliest believers life in Christ meant life in the Spirit, and that meant life characterized by power, not simply by some quiet, pervasive force. The coming of the Spirit had phenomenological evidence; life was characterized by a dynamic quality, evidenced as often as not by extraordinary phenomena. The Spirit was not someone one believed in or about; he was experienced, powerfully experienced in the life of the church, as is

---

[11] See especially the synonymous parallelism in Luke 1:35:
The *Holy Spirit* will come upon you,
and the *power of the most high* will overshadow you.
Cf. the promises in Luke 24:49 and Acts 1:4–5; where the same interchange takes place. Thus in Luke 5:17, the "power" that was present with Jesus to heal is clearly the Spirit.

vividly clear in Acts 1:8, "You shall receive power when the Holy Spirit comes upon you"; Acts 4:33, "with great power the apostles gave witness to the resurrection"; and throughout Acts. On the day of Pentecost what happened to the first Christians was something one could see and hear (Acts 2:33); it was the visible, phenomenological dimension of the Spirit that Simon wanted to buy (Acts 8); and in Cornelius' household the coming of the Spirit visibly and phenomenologically is what convinced Peter and his companions that the Gentiles too had received the promise of life. Such a view of the Spirit was normal for them. Indeed that such is the presupposition of the early church is the only way one can make sense of 1 Thessalonians 5:19–22, 1 Corinthians 12–14, and Galatians 3:5. These are not isolated occurrences, anymore than the Lord's Supper is an isolated occurrence in the Pauline churches. It was the abuse, or distortion, of what was *normal* that called for the corrective.

Thus the Spirit was not only the essential matter of the early believers' understanding of their eschatological existence, but he was powerfully present among them. This was no false triumphalism (the Corinthian error). As with their Lord, their power was often veiled in weakness (see 1 Cor 2:1–5; 2 Cor 12:1–10), but it was manifest power nonetheless. Indeed, it was the Pentecostals' ability to read the New Testament existence so correctly, along with their frustration over the less-than-adequate norm of anemia that they experienced in their own lives and in the church around them, that led to seeking for the New Testament experience in the first place. The question, of course, is, if that was the norm, what happened to the church in the succeeding generations? It is in pursuit of that question that an understanding of the Pentecostal experience as separate and subsequent lies.

III. Some Suggested Historical Reasons for the Rise of a Separate and Subsequent Experience

The problem that most Pentecostals have with the biblical data as they have just been presented is that the data do not seem to square with their own powerful experience in the Spirit, which was not in fact a part of their conversion, or becoming a Christian, but was rather "separate from and subsequent to" that conversion. Is their experience then not biblical? Or is it necessary to go back and reinterpret the biblical data to square it with our experience? I would argue *No* to both of those questions. On the one hand, the typical evangelical or reformed exegete who disallows a separate and subsequent experience simply must hide his or her head in the sand, ostrichlike, to deny the reality—the biblical reality—of what has happened to so many Christians. On the other hand, the Pentecostal must be wary of reforming the biblical data to fit his or her own experience. The solution, it seems to me, lies in two areas: (1) An examination of the components of Christian conversion as they emerge in the New Testament, and (2) an analysis of what happened to Christian experience once the church entered into a second and third generation of believers.

1. Without belaboring any of the points in detail, it seems to me that the components of Christian conversion that emerge from the New Testament data are five:

a. The actual conviction of sin, with the consequent drawing of the individual to Christ. This, all agree, is the prior work of the Holy Spirit that *leads* to conversion.

b. The application of the atonement in the person's life, including the forgiveness of the past, the canceling of the debt of sin. I would tend to put repentance here as a part of the response to the prior grace of God, which is also effected by the Spirit.

c. The regenerating work of the Holy Spirit that gives new birth, that brings forth the new creation.

d. The empowerment for life, with openness to gifts and the miraculous, plus obedience to mission. This is the component that Pentecostals want to make *subsequent* to numbers *a*, *b*, and *c*, and that the Protestant tradition wants to limit simply to fruit and growth, but tends at times seemingly to omit altogether.

e. The believer's response to all this is baptism in water, the offering of oneself back to God for life and service in his new age community, the church. This act obviously carries with it the rich symbolism of elements *b* and *c* (forgiveness and regeneration), but in itself effects neither.

Obviously, not all will agree with this assessment of things. But this is one New Testament scholar's understanding of the varied forms in which the biblical data come to us. The crucial item in all of this for the early church was the work of the Spirit; and element *d*, the dynamic empowering dimension with gifts, miracles, and evangelism (along with fruit and growth), was a normal part of their expectation and experience.

2. The problem lies with what happened to element *d* in the subsequent history of the church. The fact that it effectively got lost can scarcely be denied. Christian life came to consist of conversion without empowering, baptism without obedience, grace without love. Indeed the whole Calvinist-Arminian debate is predicated on this reality, that people can be in the church, but evidence little or nothing of the work of the Spirit in their lives. Cheap grace, Bonhoeffer called it. That such so-called Christian life exists not only cannot be denied, but one may have ruefully to admit that it represents the vast majority of believers in the history of the church. However, surely no one will argue that such *should* be the norm—even if it is now quite normal. The question is, how did such an understanding of Christian life and experience come into existence?

The answer seems to be twofold: First, it needs to be noted that the New Testament documents are for the most part all written to first generation adult converts and therefore simply do not describe or address the needs of the second and third generations. What we have described above as the normal Christian experience was normal for *converts*, those about whom the Acts is written and to whom Paul's letters were written. But for a second or third generation, who grow up in Christian homes, conversion is seldom so life-changing—nor, would I argue, can it or necessarily should it be so. But what happens is that the dynamic, experiential quality of the Christian life, as life in the Spirit, also seems to be the first element to go. Thus there arose a generation that "never knew about the empowering of the Holy Spirit."

Second, and by far the more devastating, was the eventual tie of the gift of the Spirit to water baptism, a tie that one is hard-pressed to find in any of the biblical data.[12] And then when baptism is eventually transferred from adult converts to infants in Christian homes, which meant that they, too, had

---

[12] This has been demonstrated especially in the exegesis by Dunn in his *Baptism in the Holy Spirit* [cf. my article on "Pauline Literature," in S. Burgess, G. McGee, eds., *Dictionary of Pentecostal and Charismatic Movements* (Grand Rapids: Zondervan, 1988) 675–76].

now received the Spirit, the phenomenological, experiential dimension to life in the Spirit was all but eliminated.

The result was the unfortunate omission of this valid, biblical dimension of Christian life from the life of most Christians in the subsequent history of the church. And it was in response to this sub-normal Christian experience that one is to understand most pietistic movements within Christendom, from Montanism at the end of the second century through the charismatic movement in the latter half of the twentieth. It is precisely out of such a background that one is to understand the Pentecostal movement with its deep dissatisfaction with life in Christ without life in the Spirit and their subsequent experience of a mighty baptism in the Spirit. If their timing was off as far as the biblical norm was concerned, their experience itself was not. What they were recapturing for the church was the empowering dimension of life in the Spirit as the normal Christian life.

That this experience was for them usually a separate experience in the Holy Spirit and subsequent to their conversion is in itself probably irrelevant. Given their place in the history of the church, how else might it have happened? Thus the Pentecostal should probably not make a virtue out of necessity. At the same time, neither should others deny the validity of such experience on biblical grounds, unless, as some do, they wish to deny the reality of such an empowering dimension of life in the Spirit altogether. But such a denial, I would argue, is actually an exegeting *not* of the biblical texts but of one's own experience in this later point in church history and a making of that experience normative. I for one like the biblical norm better; at this point the Pentecostals have the New Testament clearly on their side.

8

LAOS AND LEADERSHIP UNDER THE NEW COVENANT: SOME EXEGETICAL AND HERMENEUTICAL OBSERVATIONS ON CHURCH ORDER[1]

The New Testament is full of surprises, but perhaps none is so surprising as its generally relaxed attitude toward church structures and leadership; especially so, when one considers how important this issue became for so much of later church history, beginning as early as Ignatius of Antioch. Indeed, for most people the concept of "church history" refers primarily to its history as a body politic, involving both its evangelism and growth and its intellectual/theological development.

[1] This paper was originally prepared for discussion at a Regent College faculty retreat. Rather than a research paper that tries to take account of the vast array of secondary literature (on church order and laity), I have attempted something more modest: an essay that offers one NT scholar's reading of the biblical texts on specific issues related to the church as the people of God, namely, the interrelationships between people, clergy, ministry, and church order. Although what I do here is akin to re-inventing the wheel, it is hoped that some items will be fresh—although on others I can be easily scored for not having consulted the literature. I am grateful to my Regent colleagues for a vigorous discussion of the paper, from which I have made a few revisions and added some footnotes for greater clarity.

Probably for a variety of reasons,[2] the New Testament documents simply do not carry a concern for church order as an agendum.[3] The thesis of this essay is that the *primary* reason for this stems from their understanding of what it means to be the people of God under a new covenant, as that in turn is related to their common experience of the eschatological Spirit.[4] The burden of the essay is ultimately hermeneutical— how we move from the first-century documents to twentieth- (twenty-first) century application. But those questions, as always, must first be subject to the exegetical ones—how we understand the texts themselves.

I. The Issue(s)

Historically the church seems to have fallen into[5] a model that eventually developed a sharp distinction between

---

[2] One reason not otherwise noted in this paper is the especially ad hoc nature of our documents. Even the so-called Pastoral Epistles show little interest in church leadership or governance as such. Rather, Paul is concerned with the character and qualifications of those who assume positions of leadership. See G. D. Fee, *1 and 2 Timothy*, 19–23, 78–79.

[3] As I have noted elsewhere, the very fact that such diverse groups as Roman Catholics, Plymouth Brethren, and Presbyterians all use the Pastoral Epistles to support their ecclesiastical structures should give us good reason to pause as to what the NT "clearly teaches" on these matters. See "Reflections on Church Order in the Pastoral Epistles, with Further Reflection on the Hermeneutics of ad hoc Documents," *JETS* 28 (1985) 141–51. This is one of the things that makes Acts such a different kind of "church history" from its successors. There is scarcely a hint of church organization or structures (1:15–26 and 6:1–6 play quite different roles). At some point, for example, leadership in Jerusalem passed from the Twelve to James (cf. 6:2 and 8:14 with 11:2; 12:17; and 15:13), without so much as a word as to how or why. At the local level, in 13:1–3, those who appear to be in leadership are "prophets and teachers," while in 14:23 elders are appointed for each congregation. This is hardly the stuff from which one can argue with confidence as to how the early church was "organized"—or whether it was!

[4] By this I mean something quite technical, namely, the out-pouring of the promised Holy Spirit as the primary reality indicating that Jewish eschatological hopes had been fulfilled, or realized. For the early church "this is that which was spoken by the prophet Joel" (Acts 2:16), the sure evidence that the End (Eschaton) had begun and the time of the future had dawned.

[5] In contrast to having come by such order through purposeful, intentional action on its part.

the people themselves (laity) and the professional ministry (clergy), reaching its sharpest expression in the Roman Catholic communion,[6] but finding its way into almost every form of Protestantism as well. The net result has been a church in which the clergy all too often exist apart from the people, for whom there is a different set of rules and different expectations, and a church in which the "gifts" and "ministry," not to mention significance, power structures, and decision-making are the special province of the professionals. Being "ordained" to this profession, the latter tend to like the aura that it provides, and having such ordained professionals allows the laity to pay them to do the work of the ministry and thus excuse themselves from their biblical calling. The rather universal model, with a few exceptions, looks something like this:

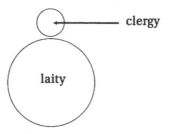

Figure 8.1 Contemporary Ecclesiastical Structure

The biblical model, on the other hand, looks something far more like the following diagram—without clergy at all, but with *identifiable leadership,* who were simply *part of the whole people of God:*

Figure 8.2 Biblical Leadership Model

[6] I mean *de jure,* of course. One of my colleagues pointed out that *de facto* there is nothing more severe in this regard than some independent churches (baptist, pentecostal/charismatic).

The problem for most moderns, of course, in coming to the biblical texts, is that we tend to presuppose our resultant form of church to be theirs; we therefore carry both different agenda and a different experience of the church back to the documents. But history and tradition have had their innings. Even though it is arguable that we have genuine continuity with the New Testament church in many ways—especially our experience of grace and the Spirit—our experience of the church itself is so far different from theirs that seemingly ne'er the twain shall meet.[7]

As I see it, the areas of difficulty are four: (1) the tension between individual and corporate life, where Western Christians in particular are trained from birth to value the individual above the group, whereas in the New Testament perspective the community is still the primary reality, and the individual finds identity and meaning as part of the community; (2) the tension between eschatological and institutional existence, most moderns knowing only the latter, whereas the New Testament church existed primarily as an experience of the former; (3) the place of structures as they flow out of these two tensions; and (4) the hermeneutical difficulty created by the nature of data, since the New Testament documents, which teem with reflections and insights, have very little directly intentional instruction on these matters. So how do they apply? Do we seek a biblical norm to follow,[8] or seek to model what fits our situation best, or try rather to approximate the spirit of the biblical pattern in our already existing structures?

---

[7] For me this is always brought home as a living reality in teaching NT theology. Although my emphases and packaging of the biblical data frequently stimulate rousing discussion (debate?), nothing does so quite as much as the section in Pauline theology on the nature of the church as the eschatological people of God, presently living out the life of the future as they await the consummation. Not only do I have great difficulty in helping students to catch the NT perspective, but even when it happens, there is difficulty in assimilating it—because this touches them right where they live.

[8] Whether we should try to model the NT church, of course, is yet another hermeneutical question in its own right. On the place of "historical precedent" in Christian hermeneutics, see some programmatic suggestions in Fee and Stuart, *How to Read,* 87–102. [Cf. chapter 6 in the present volume.]

I propose in the rest of this essay to take up some of these issues by first examining the biblical data and then by offering some brief hermeneutical observations in light of those data.

II. The People of God in the New Testament

1. The Language

By first pursuing the New Testament language for the Christian communities, I hope to demonstrate two realities about them: (a) their strong sense of *continuity* with the people of God under the former covenant, and (b) their basically *corporate* nature.

That the early believers thought in terms of continuity is writ large on nearly every page, in nearly every document.[9] They did not see themselves as the *"new* people of God," but as the "people of God *newly constituted."* Nowhere is this more clear than in their adopting Old Testament "people of God" language, a language appropriation that is as varied as it is thoroughgoing.

a. *Church (ekklēsia).* Because this word does not appear in the English Old Testament, and because its usage for the "assembly" of the Greek *polis* is generally well known, the Old Testament background for New Testament usage is frequently overlooked. In the Septuagint (LXX) *ekklēsia* is regularly used to translate the Hebrew *qahal,* referring most often to the "congregation of Israel," especially when it was gathered for religious purposes.[10] Thus this word in particular was a natural one for the early believers to bridge the gap as they began to spill over into the Gentile world.

---

[9] This is no more than we should expect, given Jesus as the fulfillment of Jewish messianic expectations, his own announcement of the kingdom as "fulfilling the time," and the Jewish complexion of the earliest believers. Continuity is thus found in a whole variety of ways in the Gospels: e.g., in direct statements reflecting the motif of promise and fulfillment, in symbols and images of various kinds (Jesus' choice of the Twelve is scarcely accidental!), in the hymns in Luke's birth narrative.

[10] Thus, e.g., Deut 31:30: "And Moses recited the words of this song from beginning to end in the hearing of the whole *ekklēsia* of Israel."

Since the concept of a "gathered people" was primary in both Greek and LXX usage, it is arguable that this is what lay behind the earliest Christian usage as well. Thus in its first appearance in the New Testament (1 Thess 1:1) Paul is probably thinking primarily of the Christian community as a gathered people, constituted "in God the Father and the Lord Jesus Christ," who would be listening to the letter as it was read. It is also arguable that its usage throughout the New Testament never gets very far away from this nuance; the *ekklēsia* refers first of all to the people in the various cities and towns who gather regularly in the name of the Lord for worship and instruction.

b. *People (laos)*. Although not particularly popular with Greek writers, this is the word chosen by the LXX translators[11] to render the Hebrew *'am*, the word that occurs most often (over 2000 times) to express the special relationship Israel had with Yahweh: Above all else they were Yahweh's "people." Although at times the word can distinguish the people (usually non-Israelite) from their leaders (e.g., Gen 41:40; Exod 1:22), in most cases it is the collective word that designates the whole people whom God had chosen—people, priests, prophets, and kings together. Thus in Exodus 19:5, in establishing his covenant with them at Sinai, God says (LXX), "You shall be for me a *laos periousios* (special/chosen people) from among the *ethnon* (nations/Gentiles)."

In the New Testament the word occurs most often to refer to the Jewish people of that era.[12] But in several striking passages it is used in its Old Testament sense, especially reflecting the language of Exodus 19:5–6 (cf. 23:22 LXX), to refer to people of the new covenant, usually in contexts that include Gentiles. Thus Luke reports James as saying: "How God at first showed his concern by taking from the *ethnon* a *laos* for his name" (Acts 15:14); in 2 Corinthians 6:16 Paul, by way of Old Testament citation, specifically applies "people of God" language to God's new temple, the church; in Titus 2:14 the goal

[11] Probably because the more common word *ethnos* was used by Greek writers to refer to themselves as a people in the same way the Hebrews used *'am*. Thus for the Jews *ethnos* came to equal "Gentiles," and was so used by the LXX translators. Hence the need for a different word to distinguish themselves.

[12] Luke uses it most often (84 of 142); Matthew 14; Hebrews 13; Paul 12; Revelation 9. In many of these it occurs in citations of the OT.

of Christ's saving purpose is "that he might purify for himself a *laos periousios,*" while 1 Peter 2:9–10 combines "people" language from two Old Testament passages (Isa 43:20/Exod 19:6/ Isa 43:21), followed by a word play on Hosea 2:25 (cf. 1:9), to designate Gentile Christians as "a chosen people, a royal priesthood, a holy nation, a people belonging to God," who were formerly "no people" but now "are the people of God." So also the author of Hebrews transfers several Old Testament "people" passages or concepts to the church (2:17; 4:9; 7:27; 13:12).

c. *Covenant (diathēkē).* Although this term does not occur often in the New Testament, it is used in ways that are significant to our topic. The author of Hebrews in particular adopts covenantal language to tie the new to the old, seeing Christ as the fulfillment of Jeremiah's "new covenant" in which God says again, as in the sinaitic covenant, "They shall be for me a people" (Heb 8:7–12; citing Jer 31:34). Paul also adopts this language to refer to the "new covenant" of the Spirit (2 Cor 3:6; cf. Gal 4:24). Perhaps even more significantly, as the people joined in common fellowship at the Table of the Lord in the Pauline churches, they did so with these words: "This cup is the new covenant in my blood" (1 Cor 11:25; Luke 22:20). It should be noted that both the language "new covenant" and its close tie with the Spirit and the people of God are seen in terms of continuity with the Old Testament (in this case as fulfillment); thus in the church's earliest worship and liturgy there was the constant reminder of their continuity/discontinuity with the past.[13]

d. *Saints (hoi hagioi).* Although not frequent in the Old Testament, the designation of Israel as God's "holy people" occurs in the crucial covenantal passage in Exodus 19:5–6, an expression that in later Judaism referred to the elect who were to share in the blessings of the messianic kingdom (Dan 7:18– 27; Ps Sol 17; Qumran). This is Paul's primary term for God's newly formed, eschatological people. He uses it in the salutation of six of the nine letters addressed to congregations, plus Philemon, as well as in several other kinds of settings. Its

---

[13] Just as the Lord's Table, through its symbol of the bread (1 Cor 10:16–17), should serve for us as a reminder of our continuity with centuries of believers.

appearance in Acts 9:41; Hebrews 6:10; 13:24; Jude 3; and
Revelation 8:4 makes it clear that this was widespread usage
in the early church. In all cases it is a designation for the collective people of God, who are to bear his "holy" character
and thus to be "set apart" for his purposes. To put that another way, the New Testament knows nothing about individual "saints," only about Christian communities as a whole
who take up the Old Testament calling of Israel to be "God's
holy people" in the world.[14]

    e. *Chosen (eklektos and cognates)*. Closely related to
the covenant is the concept of Israel as having been chosen by
God, by an act of sheer mercy on his part. In the Old Testament
this concept is most often found in verb form, with God as the
subject. However, the LXX of Isaiah 43:20–21 uses *eklektos* as
a designation for the restored people of God. This usage is
picked up in several places in the New Testament (e.g., Mark
13:22; 1 Thess 1:4; 2 Thess 2:13; Col 3:12; Eph 1:4,11; 1 Pet 1:2;
2:9). As in the Old Testament the term refers not to individual
election, but to a people who have been chosen by God for his
purposes; as one has been incorporated into, and thus
belongs to, the chosen people of God, one is in that sense also
elect. Likewise in the Old Testament, this language places the
ultimate ground of our being in a sovereign and gracious God,
who willed and initiated salvation for his people.

    f. *Royal Priesthood.* This term, taken directly from Exo-
dus 19:6, is used in 1 Peter 2:9–10 to refer to the church. I
include it here not only because it is further demonstration of
continuity, but also because as in the Exodus passage it so
clearly refers to the people corporately,[15] not to individual
priests or to the priesthood of individual believers.[16]

---

[14] See G. D. Fee, *First Corinthians*, 32–33, for the difficulties in
rendering this term into English; the option which seems best to cap-
ture its inherent nuances is "God's holy people."

[15] Cf. B. Childs on Exod 19:6: "Israel as a people is also dedicated to God's service among the nations as priests function with a
society" (*The Book of Exodus* [Philadelphia: Westminster, 1974] 367).

[16] The NT knows nothing of the "priesthood of the believer" as it
is popularly conceived, with each person's being his or her own priest with
God, without need of an external priesthood. To the contrary, the NT teaches
that the church has a priestly function for the world (1 Pet 2:9–10); and our
role of ministering to one another makes us priests one for another.

g. *The Israel of God.* This unique expression occurs only in Galatians 6:16 in the entire Bible. Nonetheless, in many ways it gathers up much of the New Testament thinking—especially Paul's—on this matter. All those who live by the "rule" that neither circumcision nor uncircumcision counts for anything, these are "the Israel of God" upon whom God's benediction of shalom and mercy now rests.[17] While it is true that Paul does not call the church the "new Israel," such passages as Romans 2:28–29; 9:6; Philippians 3:3, and this one demonstrate that Paul saw the church as the "true Israel," i.e., as in the true succession of the Old Testament people of God. At the same time it emphasizes that those people are now newly constituted—composed of Jew and Gentile alike, and based solely on faith in Christ and the gift of the Spirit.

This comes through nowhere more forcefully than in the argument of Galatians itself, for which this passage serves as the climax. Paul's concern throughout has been to argue that through Christ and the Spirit Gentiles share with believing Jews full privileges in the promises made to Abraham (indeed are Abraham's true children), without submitting to Torah in the form of Jewish identity symbols (circumcision, food laws, calendar observance).[18] They do *not* need to submit to the regulations of the old covenant in order to be full members of the people of God; indeed, in "belonging to Christ," they are "Abraham's seed, and heirs according to the promise" (3:29), which is confirmed for them by the gift the Spirit (4:6–7).

Here especially the primary name for God's ancient people has been taken over in the interests of continuity, but

[17] Although it is grammatically possible that this phrase refers to Jewish people, and is so argued by many (see esp. P. Richardson, *Israel in the Apostolic Church* [SNTSMS 10; Cambridge: Cambridge University Press, 1969] 74–102), both the unusual nature of the qualifier "of God" and the context of the whole argument argue for the position taken here.
[18] The issue in Galatians is not first of all justification by faith (i.e., entrance requirements), but whether Gentiles, who have already been justified by faith in Christ and given the Spirit must also submit to Jewish boundary markers (i.e., maintenance requirements) in order to share in the covenant with Abraham (as Gen 17:1–14 makes so clear). For arguments presenting this perspective see T. David Gordon, "The Problem in Galatia," *Interpretation* 41 (1987) 32–43; and J. D. G. Dunn, "The Theology of Galatians," *SBL 1988 Seminar Papers* (Atlanta: Scholars Press, 1988) 1–16.

now predicated on new terms. The Israel *of God* includes both Jew and Gentile, who by faith in Christ and "adoption" by the Spirit have become Abraham's "free children," and through Christ they have become the inheritors of the promises made to Abraham. Gentile believers *as a people* are included in the newly constituted people of God, the Israel of God, which is at the same time also an obviously corporate image.

h. *Further (Non-Old Testament) Images.* The essentially corporate nature of the people of God is further demonstrated by the various images for the church found in the New Testament that are *not* from the Old Testament: *family*, where God is Father and his people are brothers and sisters (2 Cor 6:18); the related image of *household*, where the people are members of the household (1 Tim 3:5,15) and their leaders the Master's servants (1 Cor 4:1–3); *body*, where the emphasis is simultaneously on their unity and diversity (1 Cor 10:17; 12:12–26); God's *temple*, or sanctuary, where by the Spirit they corporately serve as the place of God's dwelling (1 Cor 3:16–17; 2 Cor 6:16; Eph 2:21–22); God's *commonwealth*, where as citizens of heaven Jew and Gentile alike form a *polis* in exile, awaiting their final homeland (Phil 3:20–21; Eph 2:19; 1 Pet 1:1,17).

In sum: By using so much Old Testament language to mark off its own identity, the early church saw itself not only as in continuity with the Old Testament people of God, but as in the true succession of that people. One of the essential features of this continuity is the corporate nature of the people of God. God chose, and made covenant with, not individual Israelites but with a people, who would bear his name and be for his purposes. Although individual Israelites could forfeit their position in Israel, this never affected God's design or purposes with the people as a people. This is true even when the majority failed, and the "people" were reduced to a "remnant." That remnant was still Israel—loved, chosen, and redeemed by God.

This is the thoroughgoing perspective of the New Testament as well, but at the same time Christ's coming and the gift of the eschatological Spirit also marked a new way by which they were constituted. The community is now entered individually through faith in Christ and the reception of the Spirit, signalled by baptism. Nonetheless, the church itself is the object of God's saving activity in Christ. God is thus choosing and saving a people for his name.

Perhaps nothing illustrates this quite so vividly as two passages in 1 Corinthians (5:1–13; 6:1–11), where rather flagrant sins on the part of individuals are addressed. In both cases Paul aims his heaviest artillery not at the individual sinners, but at the church for its failure to deal with the matters. In 5:1–13 the man is not so much as spoken to, and his partner is not mentioned at all; everything is directed at the church—for its arrogance, on the one hand, and its failure to act, on the other. So also in 6:1–11. In this case he does finally speak to the plaintiff (vv. 7–8a) and the defendant (vv. 8b–11), but only after he has scored the church for its allowing such a thing to happen at all among God's eschatological community, and thus for its failure to act. What is obviously at stake in these cases is the church itself and its role as God's redeemed and redemptive alternative to Corinth.

2. The People and Their Leadership

The sense of continuity with the old, however, does not seem to carry over to the role of leadership as well. Under the old covenant the king and priests in particular, although often included in much of the "people" language, were at the same time recognized as having an existence apart from the people, with their own sets of rules and expectations. It is precisely this model of leadership that breaks down altogether in the New Testament. The basic reason for this is the Lordship of Christ himself. As God intended to be himself king over Israel, so Christ has come as God's king over his newly constituted people. As head of his church, all others, including leaders, function as parts of the body both sustained by Christ and growing up into him (Eph 4:11–16).[19]

[19] [Surely one of the ironies of my own tradition, the American Assemblies of God, as well as that of many other such traditions is that every criticism of the ministry in any of its forms, including very bad preaching, was always challenged on the basis of 1 Sam 24:6, "The Lord forbid that I should do this thing to my lord, the Lord's anointed." Although Pentecostals might argue that the NT analogy of "the Lord's anointed" is the one who speaks by the Spirit, in fact this became a tacit elevation of "ordained" ministry to the position of the untouchable

Thus leadership in the New Testament people of God is never seen as outside or above the people themselves, but simply as part of the whole, essential to its well-being, but governed by the same set of "rules." They are not "set apart" by "ordination";[20] rather, their gifts are part of the Spirit's work among the whole people. That this is the basic model (as diagrammed earlier) can be demonstrated in a number of ways, some of which deserve special attention.

a. *The Nature of the Epistles.* One of the more remarkable features of the New Testament Epistles is the twin facts (a) that they are addressed to the church(es) as a whole, not to the church leadership,[21] and (b) that leaders, therefore, are seldom, if ever,[22] singled out either to see to it that the directives of a given letter are carried out or to carry the directives out themselves. To the contrary, in every case, the writers address the community as a whole, and the expectation of the letter is that there will be a community response to the directives. In

king. No wonder the history of such movements, and even more so of independent churches, is fraught with stories of ministerial moral failure. Kings play by a different set of rules, and the structures of accountability are seldom in place.]

[20] That is, they are not "set apart" to an *office*; rather, hands are laid upon them in recognition of the Spirit's prior activity. Cf. Acts 13:1–2; 1 Tim 4:4.

[21] The one exception to this is Philippians, where Paul writes to the church "together with the overseers and deacons." One might also include Philemon, where Paul includes Archippus in the salutation, but since the letter is addressed to Philemon, Paul continues by mentioning two further individuals before including the church. Some, of course, would argue that 1 Timothy and Titus are such documents; however, both of these younger colleagues serve as Paul's own apostolic delegates in Ephesus and Crete. They are both itinerants, whose stay is temporary. Thus they are not church leaders in the local sense.

[22] One exception to this might be Col 4:17, where Paul specifically tells the church to exhort Archippus to "complete the task you have received in the Lord" (NRSV); but even here the church is the primary focus, and it is not at all clear what Archippus' "task" is. Cf. Phil 4:3, where Paul asks a trusted fellow-worker to mediate the differences between Euodia and Syntyche. But in this case, since these two women are also designated as his fellow-workers, Paul is asking for help not so much from a church leader as such, but from one who has been a co-laborer with both Paul and these women. As in the preceding note, Timothy and Titus are "leaders" of a different kind. They are in their respective situations in Paul's place; they are not local leaders "in charge" of the church.

several instances leaders are mentioned (e.g., 1 Thess 5:12–13; 1 Cor 16:16; Heb 13:17), but basically in order to address the community's attitudes toward them. In 1 Peter 5:1–4 the leaders themselves (apparently)[23] are addressed, in this case with regard to their attitudes and responsibilities toward the rest of the people.

Thus, for example, in 1 Thessalonians 5:12–13 the whole community is called upon, among other things, to respect those who labor among them, care for them,[24] and admonish them; yet in vv. 14–15, when urging that they "admonish the idle, encourage the fainthearted, help the weak, be patient with all," Paul is once more addressing *the community as a whole,* not its leadership in particular. So also in 2 Thessalonians 3:14 the whole community is to "note that person" who does not conform to Paul's instruction and "have nothing to do with him." Likewise, in all of 1 Corinthians not one of the many directives is spoken to the leadership, and in 14:26 their worship is singularly corporate in nature ("When you [plural] assemble together, *each one of you* has . . . ; let all things be done with an eye to edification"). One receives the distinct impression that people and leaders alike are under the sovereign direction of the Holy Spirit.

This is not to downplay the role of leadership;[25] rather, it is to recognize that in the New Testament documents leaders are always seen as *part of the whole people of God,* never as a group unto themselves. Hence they "labor among" you, Paul

---

[23] This seems almost certainly to be the case, despite the corresponding "younger men" that follows in v. 5.

[24] The verb in this case is ambiguous in Greek, meaning either to "govern" or to "care for." Apart from 1 Tim 3:4–5, elsewhere in the NT, as here, it is used absolutely so that one cannot determine which nuance is intended. But in the Timothy passage the synonym that is substituted for it in v. 5 means unambiguously to "care for." This seems most likely what Paul ordinarily had in mind. Cf. E. Best, *The First and Second Epistles to the Thessalonians* (San Francisco: Harper & Row, 1972) 224–25.

[25] Indeed, despite some NT scholarship to the contrary, it is highly unlikely that the early communities ever existed long without local leadership. The picture Luke gives in Acts 14:23 is an altogether plausible one historically, given the clear evidence of leadership in the earliest of the Pauline letters (1 Thess 5:12–13)—a community where he had not stayed for a long time, whose leadership must have been in place when he was suddenly taken from them (Acts 17:10; 1 Thess 2:17).

repeatedly says, and their task in Ephesians 4:11–16 is especially "to prepare God's people ['the saints'] for works of service ['ministry'], so that the body of Christ may be built up." Thus the model that emerges in the New Testament is not that of clergy and laity, but of the whole people of God, among whom the leaders function in service of the rest.

All of this is quite in keeping with Jesus' word that his disciples were to call no one "rabbi," "father," or "master," for "you have one teacher and you are all brothers and sisters" (Matt 23:8–12), and with his word that "those who are supposed to rule over the Gentiles lord it over them, and their great men exercise authority over them. But it shall not be so among you; but whoever would be great among you must be your servant, and whoever would be first among you must be slave of all" (Mark 10:42–44).

b. *The New Testament Imperatives.* Closely related to this is another reality that is easily missed in an individualistic culture, namely, that the imperatives in the Epistles are primarily corporate in nature and have to do first of all with the community and its life together; they address individuals only as they are part of the community. In the early church everything was done *allelōn* ("one another"). They were members of one another (Rom 12:5; Eph 4:25),[26] who were to build up one another (1 Thess 5:11; Rom 14:19), care for one another (1 Cor 12:25), love one another (1 Thess 3:12; 4:9; Rom 13:8; 1 John passim), bear with one another in love (Eph 4:2), bear one another's burdens (Gal 6:2), be kind and compassionate to one another, forgive one another (Eph 4:32), submit to one another (Eph 5:21), consider one another better than themselves (Phil 2:3), be devoted to one another in love (Rom 12:10), and live in harmony with one another (Rom 12:16).

All of the New Testament imperatives are to be understood within this framework. Unfortunately, many texts which Paul intended for the community as a whole have been regularly individualized, thus losing much of their force and impact. For example, in 1 Corinthians 3:10–15 Paul is not talking

---

[26] This is an obvious reference to the imagery of the church as the body of Christ, another corporate image used by Paul, which I have not dealt with in this essay because it is both so obvious and lacking OT roots.

of believers' building their individual lives on Christ; rather, the admonition in v. 10 ("let each one take care how he/she builds") is intended precisely for those in Corinth responsible for building the church, that they do it with the imperishable materials compatible with the foundation (a crucified Messiah), not with "wisdom" and division. Likewise vv. 16–17 are a warning to those who would "demolish" God's temple, the church in Corinth, by their divisions and fascination with "wisdom." And on it goes. "Work out your own salvation with fear and trembling, for God is at work in you both to will and to work for his good pleasure" (Phil 2:12–13) is not a word to the individuals in the community to work harder at their Christian lives, but is spoken to a community that is out of sync with one another (as vv. 1–5 make clear) and that needs to work out its common salvation with God's help. In the same vein, it is impossible to compute the misunderstandings that have arisen over 1 Corinthians 12–14 because the text has been looked at outside the context of the community at worship.

All of this, then, to say that the people of God in the New Testament are still thought of corporately, and they are addressed individually only as they are members of the community. And leadership is always seen as part of the whole complex. Leaders do not exercise authority over God's people— although the community is to respect them and submit to their leadership; rather, they are the "servants of the farm" (1 Cor 3:5–9), or "household" (1 Cor 4:1–3). The New Testament is not concerned with their place in the governance structures (hence as we will note below, we know very little about these), but with their attitudes and servant nature. They do not rule,[27] but serve and care for—and that within the circle, as it were.

III. The Theological Basis for the New Testament People of God

Before turning our attention to some observations about the nature of structures and ministry in the New Testament, it is time now to suggest the theological/experiential basis for

[27] Language of "rulership" and "authority" is altogether missing in the NT passages which speak about leadership, except as Paul refers to his apostolic authority in his own churches.

the New Testament church's *discontinuity* with the old, and thus for their being a newly constituted people, which in turn accounts for their relaxed attitude toward governance structures as such. This basis, I suggest, is a combination of three realities:[28] the work of Christ, the gift of the Spirit, and the eschatological framework within which both of these were understood.

1. The Work of Christ

We need not belabor this point. The single, central reality of the New Testament is that "God has made him both Lord and Christ, this Jesus whom you crucified" (Acts 2:36); and that changes everything. On the one hand, he "fulfills" all manner of hopes and expectations, thus functioning as both continuity and discontinuity with the old: he is the "seed" of Abraham, inheritor of the promises to Abraham, through whom both Jew and Gentile alike are now "heirs according to promise" (Gal 3:16, 29); he is the great high priest, whose singular sacrifice of himself eliminates all other priests and offerings, through whom we all now have direct access to the Father (Hebrews); he is the rejected stone now become the chief cornerstone by whom we have become living stones in God's new "spiritual house" (1 Pet 2:4–8).

On the other hand, the death and resurrection of Christ bring an *end* to the old and begin the new. His death ratified a new covenant, so that the people of God are newly constituted—based on faith in Christ and including Gentile as well as Jew.[29] His resurrection set the future in motion in such a way that this newly constituted people are "raised with him"

---

[28] To be complete and more precise, of course, one should start with their absolutely primary theological presupposition: That the one God—holy, sovereign, and gracious—had purposed their salvation, which he effected in Christ and made available for all through the Spirit (see e.g., Gal 4:4–7).

[29] The classic illustration of Paul's own struggle with continuity and discontinuity between the new and the old—expressed in terms of Gentile and Jew—is Romans 11, where Gentiles have been grafted onto the olive tree "and now share in the nourishing sap from the olive root" (v. 17, NIV). Yet Israel itself must be regrafted in order to be saved.

and enter an entirely new mode of existence—so much so that a radical new understanding of that existence also emerged.

This is obviously the focus of New Testament theology, and the primary reason for discontinuity with the former people of God (in the sense that they must now come through Christ in order to belong). But such focus does not in itself account for the people of God sensing themselves to be a *newly constituted people* as well.[30] This can only be accounted for on the basis of the eschatological framework of their self-understanding and the role of the Spirit within that understanding.

2. The Gift of the Spirit

Although the New Testament people of God were constituted on the basis of Christ's death and resurrection, the Spirit, who appropriated that work to their lives, was the key to their *present* existence as that people. The Spirit is both the *evidence* that God's eschatological future had dawned (Acts 2:16–21) and the *guarantee* of their own inheritance at its consummation (Eph 1:13–14).[31] The Spirit is that which marks off God's people from the rest, whereby they understand the wisdom of the cross, which the world counts as foolishness

---

[30] After all, in the early going, as Luke portrays things in Acts 1–6, the early believers lived within Judaism—and surely expected that all Jewry would acknowledge Jesus as Messiah, Savior, and Lord.

[31] Cf. the powerful eschatological metaphors of the Spirit in Paul that especially make these double points: "seal" (2 Cor 1:21–22; Eph 1:13; 4:30); "earnest/first installment" (2 Cor·2:21–22; 5:5; Eph 1:14); "firstfruits" (Rom 8:23). This latter metaphor in particular helps us to see how Paul views life in the Spirit as lived in the eschatological tension of the "already" and the "not yet"; while at the same time the Spirit is the guarantee of our certain future. The larger context of Rom 8:12–27 is especially noteworthy. With the Spirit playing the leading role, Paul in vv. 15–17 has struck the dual themes (1) of our present position as children, who are thus joint-heirs with Christ of the Father's glory, and (2) of our present existence as one of weakness and suffering, as we await that glory. These are the two themes taken up in vv. 18–27. By the Spirit we have already received our "adoption" as God's children, but what is "already" is also "not yet"; therefore, by the same Spirit, who functions for us as *firstfruits*, we await our final "adoption as children, the redemption of our bodies." The first sheaf is God's pledge to us of the final harvest.

(1 Cor 2:6–16). Their common experience of Spirit, both Jew and Gentile, plus their continuing experience of the Spirit's activities among them, is that to which Paul appeals in Galatia as evidence of the new expression of being God's people (Gal 3:2–5); and the Spirit by whom they walk, in whom they live, and by whom they are led is the reason they no longer need Torah (5:16–23). Not only has Christ brought an end to Torah but by belonging to him believers have also crucified the flesh (Gal 5:24) that was aroused by Torah (Rom 7:5). Through the Spirit they fulfill the whole Torah as well as the law of Christ by loving one another (Gal 5:13–14; 6:2).

Moreover, the Spirit is the key to their existence as a people. Through Christ both Jew and Gentile together "have access in one Spirit to the Father" (Eph 2:18). By their common, lavish experience of Spirit the many of them in Corinth, with all their differences and diversity, became the one body of Christ (1 Cor 12:13); by the Spirit's abiding in/among them they form God's temple, holy unto him—set apart for his purposes as his alternative to Corinth (1 Cor 3:16–17).

Finally, the Spirit serves as the key to their new view of ministry. Ministry lies not in individuals with inherited offices, nor even in individuals with newly created offices. Ministry lies with the gifting of the Spirit. God through his Spirit has placed ministries in the church; and since the Spirit is the eschatological Spirit of Joel's prophecy, all of God's people are potential prophets—Jew/Gentile, male/female, home owner/ slave. The Spirit is unconscious of race, sex, or rank. He gifts whom he wills for the common good (1 Cor 12:7, 11).

Thus the Spirit, as available to all, and gifting various people in divers ways as he wills, is the crucial ingredient of their new self-understanding—and thus of their discontinuity with the old.

3. The Eschatological Framework

The net result of Jesus' death and resurrection followed by the advent of the Spirit was that the early church understood itself to be an eschatological community, "upon whom the end of the ages has come" (1 Cor 10:11). The early Christian's citizenship was already in heaven, from whence they were awaiting Christ's return to bring the final consummation (Phil 3:20–21). With the resurrection of Christ, God set the future inexorably in motion (1 Cor 15:20–28), so that the form of this present world is passing away (1 Cor 7:31).

Thus the early church understood the future as "already" but "not yet"[32] and its own existence as "between the times." At the Lord's Table they celebrated "the Lord's death until he comes" (1 Cor 11:26). By the resurrection and the gift of the Spirit they had been stamped with eternity. They had been "born anew to a living hope . . . to an imperishable inheritance preserved in heaven for them" (1 Pet 1:3–5). They already "sat in the heavenlies" through Christ (Eph 1:4). In their present existence, therefore, they were living the life of the future, the way things were eventually to be, as they awaited the consummation. It is thus in light of the eschatological realities of their existence that Paul tries to shame the Corinthians by trivializing both the need to redress one's grievances and the secular courts in which such litigation took place; in light of eschatological realities such things count for nothing (1 Cor 6:1–6).

As much as anything, it is this sense that Christ's death and resurrection marked the turning of the ages, and that the Spirit in / among them was God's down payment and guarantee of their future, that marked the crucial point of discontinuity with what had gone before. With Christ and the Spirit they had *already begun their existence as the future people of God*. And it is precisely this new, eschatological existence that transforms their understanding of being his people. The future has already begun; the Spirit has come upon all of the people alike, so that the only differences between / among them reflect the diversity of the Spirit's gifts, not a hierarchy of persons or offices. There can be no "kings" or "priests" in this new order, precisely because this future kingdom, which was inaugurated by Jesus and the Spirit, is the kingdom *of God*, and thus a return in an even grander way to the theocracy that was God's first order for Israel.

[32] Cf. 1 John 3:2: "Beloved, we are God's children *now*; it does *not yet* appear what we shall be, but we know that when he appears we shall be like him, for we shall see him as he is."

IV. Structure and Ministry in the New Testament

As already noted, one of the truly perplexing questions in New Testament studies is to determine the shape that leadership and structures took within the earliest congregations of God's new covenant people. The difficulties here stem from the lack of explicit, intentional instruction, noted at the beginning of this study. The reasons for it are related to the twofold reality of their eschatological existence and their experience of the Spirit, not to mention the simple fact that one seldom instructs on something that is generally a given.

What I hope to do here is to offer some reflections on the data as they come to us in the documents. Several things seem quite certain:

Leadership was of two kinds.[33] On the one hand, there were itinerants, such as the apostle Paul and others, who founded churches and exercised obvious authority over the churches they had founded. On the other hand, when the itinerant founder or his delegate were not present, leadership on the local scene seems to have been left in the hands of "elders,"[34] all expressions of which in the New Testament are plural. Thus Paul founded the church in Corinth, and it is to him that they owe their allegiance—so much so that he rather strongly denounces other "apostles" who teach foreign doctrines on his turf (cf. 2 Cor 10:12–18).

In the same vein Paul delegates Timothy, and apparently later Titus, to straighten out the mess in Ephesus created by some false teachers, who in my view were elders who had gone astray.[35] Timothy is not the "pastor"; he is there in Paul's place, exercising Paul's authority. But he is to replace the fallen elders with new ones, who will care for the church and teach when Timothy is gone (1 Tim 5:17–22; 2 Tim 2:2; 4:9). The elders in the local churches seem to have been

[33] But not of the two kinds most often noted in the literature: charismatic and regular. Rather, it is itinerant and local. Authority lies with the itinerant, except when he is on the local scene.

[34] Since the earliest congregations grew out of Judaism, the (chiefly lay) elders of the Jewish synagogues almost certainly served as the model for the early Christian communities.

[35] See Fee, *1 and 2 Timothy*, 7–10.

composed of both *episkopoi* (overseers) and *diakonoi* (deacons), who probably had different tasks; but from this distance there is little certainty as to what they were (except that the *episkopoi* were to be "capable teachers," 1 Tim 3:2).

Unless Revelation 2–3 provides an exception, there is no certain evidence in the New Testament of a single leader at the local level who was not at the same time an itinerant. The status of James in Jerusalem is at once a more vexed and complex issue. In an earlier time, as evidenced by both Luke and Paul, he appears to have been one among equals. But as the others moved on and he stayed, he apparently emerged eventually as the predominant leader, but in what capacity one is hard pressed to determine. In any case, he was not native to Jerusalem—a kind of "permanent itinerant"?—and probably exercised the kind of leadership there that Paul did over his churches.

Because of the authority vested in the apostle as founder of churches—either by the apostle himself or as in the case of Epaphras one of the apostle's co-workers—there does not seem to be any other outside authority for the local churches. That is, apostles apparently did not assume authority in churches they had not founded. Paul's considerably more restrained approach to the church in Rome in contrast to his other letters serves as evidence.

Moreover, even though there is a form of collegiality among the "apostles" and "elders," Paul at least did not consider any one of them to have authority over him, although he felt a kind of urgency that they all be in this thing together.[36] Thus, there appears to have been a kind of loose plurality at the top level, with recognition of each other's spheres and ministries as given by God (Gal 2:6–10).

Apart from the authority of the apostles over the churches they had founded, there seems to be very little interest in the question of "authority" at the local level. To be sure, the people are directed to respect, and submit to, those who labored among them and served them in the Lord (1 Cor 16:16; Heb 13:17). But the interest is not in their authority as such, but in their role as those who care for the others.

[36] Gal 2:1–10 is the clear evidence. Paul went up "by revelation" not by requirement. His urgency was a common bond in the same gospel.

The concern for governance and roles within church structures emerges at a *later* time. Nonetheless, the twofold questions of laity and women in ministry are almost always tied to this question in the contemporary evangelical debate. The great urgency always is, Who's in charge around here? which is precisely what puts that debate outside New Testament concerns.

One of the difficulties in the Pauline letters is to determine the relationship between certain gifts, especially prophecy and teaching (as e.g., in 1 Cor 14:6, 26), and people who are designated as prophets and teachers. The clear implication of 1 Corinthians 14:6 and 26–33 is that teaching, for example, is a gift that might be exercised by anyone in the community; yet in 12:28 he sets prophets and teachers after apostles as God's gifts to the community. Most likely both of these phenomena existed side by side; that is, prophesying and teaching, as well as other gifts, were regularly exercised in a more spontaneous way by any and all within the community, whereas some who exercised these gifts on a regular basis were recognized as "prophets" and "teachers." The former would be ministry for the upbuilding of the community; the latter would naturally emerge in roles of spiritual leadership within the community.

Thus, in the final analysis we know very little about the governance of either the local or larger church. That structures of some kind existed can be taken for granted; but what form these took is simply not an interest in our documents themselves. It is arguable that at least part of the reason for this is their sense of corporate life as the people of God, among whom the leaders themselves did not consider themselves "ordained" to lead the people, but "gifted" to do so as one gift among others.[37]

V. Some Hermeneutical Observations

How, then, does all—or any—of this apply to us? Here our difficulties are a mixture of several realities. First, how

---

[37] In this regard see especially how the participle for leaders "those who care for the church" is found nestled between "contributing to the needs of others" and "showing mercy" in Rom 12:8.

does one handle biblical revelation that comes to us less by direct instruction and more by our observations as to what can be gleaned from a whole variety of texts?[38] Second, if we do think in terms of "modeling" after the New Testament church, which of the various models do we opt for, and why?[39] Third, since we are already set in various traditions, and since so much water has gone under the bridge in any case, what difference does any of this make on our very real personal and corporate histories? I have no illusions that I can resolve these matters; indeed, they merely raise some of the deep hermeneutical issues that have long divided the people of God. For most of us, there is comfort in the known, and structures we are used to are easily seen as biblical. Nonetheless, I want to conclude this study with a few observations.

We should probably all yield to the reality that there are no explicitly revealed church structures that serve as the divine order for all times and in all places. Even so, I think there are *ideals* toward which we might strive—although we may very well keep present structures in place. In this regard, I would put at a top level of priority our need to model the church as an eschatological community of the Spirit, in which we think of the church as a whole people among whom leaders serve as one among many other gifts, and that one of the basic priorities of leadership is to equip and enable others for the larger ministry of the church. Despite years of ingrained "division of labor," I am convinced that a more biblical model can be effected within almost any present structure. But it will take a genuine renewal of the Holy Spirit, so that the "clergy" cease being threatened by shared gifts and ministries, and the people cease "paying the preacher to do it."

As to structures themselves, it is my guess that the model that emerged was the result of a transference of roles, in which there arose at the local level a more *permanent, single* leader, but now based on the model of the *itinerant apostle.* This bothers me none, as long as the model of a single pastor wielding great authority in the local church is not argued for as something biblical in itself. The danger with this model, of course, is that it tends to focus both authority and ministry in

[38] [On this matter see chapter 1, pp. 2–5.]
[39] [On this matter, see chapter 6, pp. 85–89.]

the hands of one or a few persons, who cannot possibly be so gifted as to fill all the needs of the local community. Furthermore, leadership, especially of the more visible kind, can be heady business. For me the great problem with single leadership is its threefold tendency to pride of place, love of authority, and lack of accountability. Whatever else, leadership in the church needs forms that will minimize these tendencies and maximize servanthood.

Thus I would urge the movement toward a more biblical view of church and leadership in which we do not eliminate "clergy"—except for all the wrong connotations that that word often brings with it—but look for a renewed leadership and people, in which ordination was not so much to an office as the recognition of the Spirit's prior gifting, and the role of leadership was more often that of Ephesians 4:11–16, preparing the whole church for its ministry to itself and to the world.

If the structures of the New Testament church themselves are not necessarily our proper goal, I would urge that the recapturing of the New Testament view of the church itself is. If the church is going to be God's genuine alternative to the world, a people truly for his name, then we must once again become an eschatological people, people who are citizens of another homeland, whose life in the Spirit is less creedal and cerebral and more fully biblical and experiential, and a people whose sense of corporate existence is so dynamic and genuine that once again it may be said of us, "How those Christians love one another."